# Trainer's Guide

*caring for*
# preschool
# children   third edition

**Diane Trister Dodge**

**Derry G. Koralek**

**Laurie Taub**

**Debra Al-Salam**

Teaching Strategies Inc.

Washington, DC

Editor: Toni S. Bickart
Cover, book design, and computer illustrations: Carla Uriona

Teaching Strategies, Inc.
P.O. Box 42243
Washington, DC 20015
www.TeachingStrategies.com
ISBN 1-879537-76-1

Teaching Strategies and *The Creative Curriculum* names and logos are registered trademarks of Teaching Strategies, Inc., Washington, DC.

The publisher and the authors cannot be held responsible for injury, mishap, or damages incurred during the use of or because of the information in this book. The authors recommend appropriate and reasonable supervision at all times based on the age and capability of each child.

Library of Congress Control Number:     2004105201

Printed and bound in the United States of America
2010      2009      2008      2007      2006      2005
10  9  8  7  6  5  4  3  2

# Table of Contents

# Introduction

*Caring for Preschool Children* is one in a series of competency-based training programs for child development center staffs and family child care providers working with children from infancy through school age. It includes two resources for teachers: *Caring for Preschool Children*, the book that contains all the readings for the 13 modules in the training program, and a *Skill-Building Journal* that guides teachers in applying what they learned from the readings and answering questions about what they learned. Each of the modules addresses the knowledge and skills related to one of the functional areas of the Child Development Associate (CDA) Competency Standards: Safe, Healthy, Learning Environment, Physical, Cognitive, Communication, Creative, Self, Social, Guidance, Families, Program Management, and Professionalism. The training program also includes this *Trainer's Guide*, which is designed for those who oversee and provide feedback to teachers as they complete the modules.

The training program introduces the core skills and knowledge of the early childhood profession. It is designed for classroom teachers who work with children ages 3–5 in private and public child care centers, Head Start, and pre-kindergarten programs. We use the term *teacher* to include classroom teachers, teacher aides and assistants, and college students.

Although there is a direct link between the training program and a developmentally appropriate curriculum, *Caring for Preschool Children* does not take the place of a curriculum. Early childhood programs should have a written curriculum that defines the program's philosophy, is based on research and theory, outlines goals for children's development and learning, and explains what children will learn (the content). The curriculum should also explain how teachers create a learning environment, guide children's learning, assess learning and development, and promote the meaningful involvement of families as partners in children's learning. All the modules in *Caring for Preschool Children* help teachers develop the skills and knowledge to effectively implement their program's curriculum.

*Caring for Preschool Children* is designed as a supervised, self-instructional training program: teachers may work on the 13 modules in any order, at their own paces, and at times that are convenient for them. Trainers play a central role in overseeing the training, tracking teachers' progress, and assessing teachers' competence. Trainers observe teachers working with children, model appropriate practices, and provide feedback and support. They review and make judgments about teachers' responses in the learning activities. When a teacher has successfully completed all the sections of a module, the trainer gives the knowledge assessments and observes the teacher to assess his or her competence in working with children, families, and colleagues.

While the training program is designed to be individualized and self-instructional, the materials are flexible enough to be used in a variety of other ways. For example, the modules can be the focus of a series of workshops offered by a training organization such as a resource and referral agency. Child development programs can use the modules as their in-house training program and discuss learning activities at staff meetings or at scheduled professional development sessions. Colleges can use selected modules in *Caring for Preschool Children* as a textbook for a range of early childhood courses.

## Key Features of the Training Program

*Caring for Preschool Children* is a unique training program. The approach incorporates several key features that are critical to its success.

**Training is individualized.** *Caring for Preschool Children* can be used by new or experienced teachers to increase their knowledge and understanding of preschool children and developmentally appropriate practice. The *Self-Assessment* and the *Pre-Training Assessments* are designed to acknowledge and build on each teacher's existing skills and knowledge. The module-completion plan (included in the Appendix) allows teachers and trainers to set individual schedules for completing the modules. The learning activities invite teachers to make choices: which child to observe, what activity to plan and implement, when to use a checklist, what part of the environment to assess and improve. Teachers are encouraged to think critically and reflect on their own performance. They also help determine when they are ready to be assessed.

**Teachers receive ongoing feedback on the basis of regular, systematic observations.** While much of the training is self-directed, the role of the trainer is critical to teachers' skill development and the application of knowledge. Trainers observe teachers working with children, give feedback based on those observations, model appropriate practices, and discuss completed learning activities.

**The training involves hands-on learning.** Most of the learning activities enable teachers to develop skills while applying knowledge on the job. Teachers develop, implement, and evaluate plans with colleagues. They build partnerships with families, use observation notes to individualize their programs, and complete checklists to identify and address problems.

**The training is competency-based.** Knowledge and competency assessments are built into the training process. The assessments provide concrete validation of each teacher's growth and learning of core competencies.

# How to Use the Trainer's Guide

The *Trainer's Guide to Caring for Preschool Children* provides guidance on using the modules for individualized training and in workshops and courses. The chapters lead trainers through the process of planning and overseeing the training program.

Chapter 1, *Planning Staff Development*, describes adult learners and the importance of counting all training toward professional development. It identifies the components of a career development system and shows how this training program leads to professional development and program improvement.

Chapter 2, *Supporting the Self-Instructional Training Process*, provides an overview of the trainer's role in introducing the training program and providing feedback to teachers as they complete each section of the modules. It describes exactly what teachers and trainers do to complete each module and suggests strategies to extend learning.

Chapter 3, *Using the Modules in Courses and Workshops*, is for trainers who will implement *Caring for Preschool Children* in group settings such as workshops, seminars, or college courses. It offers suggestions about logistics, facilitating group training sessions, varying training approaches, and evaluating the effectiveness of training. A sample outline is provided for leading a series of group training sessions on module 10, *Guidance*.

Chapter 4, *Assessing Each Teacher's Progress*, explains how to administer and score the knowledge and competency assessments and discuss the results. The *Knowledge Assessments*, *Answer Sheets*, and *Competency Assessments* are included at the end of this chapter.

The Appendix includes reproducible forms for planning the completion of modules, planning group sessions, tracking individual and group progress, documenting training, and evaluating training. There is also a certificate of completion to award to teachers when they finish all of the modules in the training program.

# Chapter 1

# Planning Staff Development

Your decision to use *Caring for Preschool Children* is a commitment to supporting the professional development of one or more classroom teachers who work with 3- to 5-year-old children. To accomplish this goal, you want the training you provide to result in increased competence and lead to career advancement for each teacher.

Effective training experiences exist within a context, not as isolated events. Just as a curriculum for young children is not simply a collection of activities, a series of workshops alone does not lead to professional growth and career advancement. The training you provide using *Caring for Preschool Children* must address core competencies and fit an established system of career development that ensures that all training experiences are documented and lead to professional development. The training should also incorporate what is known about how adults learn best.

## Considering How Adults Learn

The training design and approach for *Caring for Preschool Children* are based on adult learning principles. Most adults are self-directed and want to be responsible for their own learning. How much they get out of training depends on how important the content is to them, how much effort they put into the learning process, and whether they integrate and use what they learn. Trainers need to consider adult motivation to learn and how feedback and other forms of support reflect principles of adult learning theory.

For most adults, motivation to learn is closely related to whether they can **immediately apply the knowledge and skills** being addressed. They want to know what they will be learning so they can determine whether it will be useful. This training program defines clear objectives in the *Self-Assessment* and *Pre-Training Assessments* and at the beginning of each learning activity. At each step, teachers can clearly see what they will be learning and how it relates to their work with children.

Adults view job-related learning as a means to an end, not an end in itself. They are motivated to participate in training that allows them to **develop or improve specific job-related skills**. *Caring for Preschool Children* addresses this motivator because most of the learning activities are completed while working with children and families.

Time is a limited and valuable investment for working adults. They have more positive attitudes toward training when they believe the **time invested is well-spent**. The knowledge and skills gained through this training program will help teachers become more effective in their work with children. Trainers can reinforce this motivator by pointing out to teachers how their increased skills and knowledge are benefiting children.

A strong secondary factor related to an adult's motivation to learn is to **increase self-esteem and enjoyment of work**. This training program acknowledges and builds on what teachers already know. As they complete learning activities, modules, and the assessment process, teachers feel successful and competent. Teachers who know they are competent tend to enjoy their work and want to continue learning.

According to many studies, motivation increases with **recognition for achievements, respect for the individual as a person**, and **participation in planning and decision making**. The process for assessing teachers' knowledge and competency recognizes their accomplishments. The self-paced, individualized approach demonstrates respect for each person's unique training needs and strengths. There are many opportunities for teachers to plan and make decisions about their learning. The greatest motivation, however, is to tie training and demonstration of competence to salary increases.

## Applying the Principles of Adult Learning Theory

Effective training experiences should be based on information about how adults learn best.

Adults bring a **wealth of previous experience** to training. They find training more meaningful when their life experience is recognized and when they can relate the content to their own lives. Each *Caring for Preschool Children* module includes a section for teachers to relate the content to their own lives, and the *Pre-Training Assessments* allow them to rate their own use of strategies.

Adults need **opportunities to integrate new ideas with what they already know** so they can use the new information. Training should provide opportunities to make interpretations and draw conclusions. Many of the learning activities in this training program require teachers to answer questions about why they plan specific activities, how children react, what they might do differently in the future, and how they can build on what they learn.

Adults **acquire new concepts more slowly** than information that relates to something they already know. The self-paced nature of this training program allows enough time for teachers to learn and apply new concepts. In addition, because some learning activities build on previous ones, new concepts are repeated and reinforced.

Adults tend to **acquire information even more slowly when it conflicts with what they already know,** because it forces them to reevaluate their knowledge base. The trainer's feedback conferences with teachers are opportunities to discuss and evaluate new knowledge.

Adults tend to **take errors personally,** and some find it **difficult to take risks.** This training program encourages reflection, critical thinking, and skill development rather than focusing on right or wrong answers. Teachers are encouraged to use the *Answer Sheets* as guides for learning, rather than view them as the only correct responses.

Adults **perceive their own experiences as unique and private.** They are not always comfortable or willing to share these experiences with others. Each teacher receives a copy of the *Skill-Building Journal,* which is a personal account of that individual's professional development. Trainers need to respect teachers' privacy while offering encouragement.

Adults learn best through a **hands-on approach** that involves them actively in the learning process. The learning activities in *Caring for Preschool Children* are hands-on because they require teachers to use what they have read while caring for children and then to think and write about their experiences. Teachers' understanding is enhanced when trainers observe and provide feedback to teachers as they work with children and families.

## Applying the Principles to Training

| Principles of Adult Learning | What Trainers Can Do |
|---|---|
| Adults bring a wealth of experiences to training. | Use the *Self-Assessment* and *Pre-Training Assessments* to acknowledge what teachers already know and do. |
| Adults need time to integrate new information with what they already know. | Allow time for teachers to apply new ideas in their work and provide support and encouragement. |
| Adults need extra time to understand new information that doesn't relate to what they already know. | Respect the self-paced training approach so teachers have time to internalize new information. |
| Adults need even more time to integrate new information that conflicts with what they know. | Use feedback conferences to discuss and evaluate old and new knowledge. |
| Adults tend to take errors personally and some have difficulty taking risks. | Emphasize reflection and critical thinking rather than right or wrong answers. |
| Adults perceive their own experiences as unique and private. | Reassure teachers that the *Skill-Building Journal* is their personal record and sharing with others is their choice. |
| Adults learn best through a hands-on approach. | Observe teachers as they apply what they learn in their work with children and families. Provide support and resources for completing learning activities. |

# Making Training Count

The field of early childhood education is defined as "any part- or full-day group program in a center, school, or home that serves children from birth through age eight, including children with special developmental and learning needs."[1] It is a broad field that allows multiple entry points. Some teachers enter the profession from colleges and graduate schools with advanced degrees. Some begin preparing in high school vocational programs. Still others enter the field with no professional preparation, credential, or degree and gain professional knowledge and skills entirely on the job. Because the early childhood field includes diverse roles in a variety of settings, training experiences must accommodate many different levels of preparation, be cohesive, and lead to a credential or degree.

Today most states have established a comprehensive career development system for offering and tracking professional development experiences for early childhood educators. These organized systems ensure that all professional development experiences address the acquisition of specific skills and knowledge, lead to a certificate or credit toward a degree, and result in improved compensation and benefits. Several components of these systems are described in the chart that follows.

## A Core Body of Knowledge and Competencies

Every profession defines a specialized body of knowledge and competencies that all members of that profession are expected to have. Regardless of where they take place, training experiences for teachers of young children should address the core competencies defined by the early childhood profession.

In designing systems of professional development, most states have adopted or based their core competencies on the subject areas outlined by The Council for Professional Recognition.[2] This core body of knowledge and competencies recognizes that effective teachers of young children

- plan a safe, healthy learning environment

- advance children's physical and intellectual development

- support children's social and emotional development

- establish productive relationships with families

- manage and effective program operation

- maintain a commitment to professionalism

- observe and record children's behavior

- know and apply principles of child development and learning

These subject areas provide a blueprint for individual professional development and a way to assess progress. They are the basis for all training experiences. *Caring for Preschool Children* addresses knowledge and competencies by organizing content around the 13 functional areas defined by The Council for Professional Recognition.

## A Training Approval System

A second component of a comprehensive system of professional development is a training approval system to ensure that all training experiences meet quality standards and lead to professional development. A training approval system should include procedures for reviewing and validating workshops and conferences as eligible for continuing education units and college or graduate credit, categorizing college courses in terms of their relevance to licensing requirements and credentialing programs, and ensuring that training experiences meet requirements for specific training levels and topic areas.

In developing a training approval system, many states have followed a set of principles of effective professional development. As defined by NAEYC,[3] effective professional development experiences

- are part of an ongoing process allowing staff to continually incorporate and apply new knowledge and skills related to working with children and families

- are grounded in a sound theoretical and philosophical base and structured as a coherent and systematic program

- are responsive to an individual's background, experiences, and current role

- allow staff to see clear links between theory and practice

- use interactive, hands-on approaches that encourage staff to learn from one another

- contribute to positive self-esteem by acknowledging the skills and resources staff members bring to the training process

- provide opportunities for application and reflection and allow staff members to be observed and receive feedback about what they have learned

- encourage staff members to take responsibility for planning their own professional development program

The training approach used in *Caring for Preschool Children* reflects and builds on these principles.

To ensure that training experiences meet these principles of effective professional development, many states now require individuals who offer training as part of the career development system to be certified. The criteria used to determine certification generally include

- knowledge, education, and experience in early childhood education and child development, including areas of specialization such as special needs, that qualify them to teach the content of the class

- knowledge of how adults learn, including demonstrated sensitivity to individual differences and learning styles

- sensitivity to cultural and linguistic diversity and to one's own cultural biases

- understanding of the early childhood profession and a commitment to professionalism

- knowledge of state and local regulations and requirements for programs and staff

Organizations that offer staff training—child care agencies, Head Start programs, resource and referral agencies, Child and Adult Care Food Programs, Departments of Recreation, colleges, universities, schools—may also be required to meet criteria established by the state. Such criteria usually include ensuring that all their trainers meet established qualifications; that training meets the requirements for licensing, certification, credentialing, or a degree in early childhood education; and that the content of training is based on accepted theories and practices in early childhood education and addresses the core competencies identified by the early childhood profession. Additionally, organizations must set up a system for documenting the training provided (e.g., transcripts, certificates of attendance) and maintain a permanent record of attendance at the training sessions.

## A Personnel Registry

A third essential component of a professional development system is a centralized tracking system to document all training completed by individuals in the profession. Documentation of training can include official transcripts from a college or university, a certificate of participation from an organization providing training that is signed by the trainer or a representative from the sponsoring group, or an official form provided at a conference or training session, with appropriate safeguards to ensure validation of each person's participation. Documentation forms, such as the Training Record included in the Appendix of this *Trainer's Guide*, become part of a teacher's permanent record. Documentation must include

- the participant's name

- the title of the workshop, course, or seminar, and the competency area addressed

- training date(s)

- total number of hours of training completed, including designation of clock hours or credit hours (and the number of clock hours which constitute one credit hour)

- signature or stamp of the instructor or program administrator

A permanent registry for training records is essential to professional development for several reasons. Many states have staff training requirements built into licensing standards. Centers must keep these records, but they should also be maintained in a centralized and permanent location. Increasingly, colleges and universities give college credit for documented training experiences by certified trainers that address the profession's standards but are not part of the regular college program. Thus training experiences can lead to an AA degree, which is necessary for career development.

*Caring for Preschool Children* can be an effective tool for promoting professional growth. The 13 modules in the training program can be applied to obtaining a Child Development Associate (CDA) Credential or program accreditation.

## A CDA Credential: The First Step in Professional Development

The Child Development Associate National Credentialing Program is a major effort to provide early childhood educators with a credential based on demonstrated competency. The program began in 1971 with the goal of enhancing the quality of early childhood education by improving, evaluating, and recognizing the competence of individuals who work with children from birth to age five in center-based and family child care settings.

The Council for Professional Recognition establishes the policies and sets the standards for the credentialing program and awards the CDA Credential. The Council awards a CDA Credential to adults who demonstrate competence in caring for young children. To date, nearly 85,000 early care and education workers have received a CDA Credential.

There are two routes to obtaining a CDA Credential: Direct Assessment and the Professional Preparation Program. To apply through Direct Assessment, a candidate must document completion of 120 contact hours of training with no less than ten hours in each of the eight subject areas defined by the profession. Formal training may be provided by training specialists, Head Start or child care agencies, colleges, vocational/technical schools, or resource and referral agencies, and it must cover the specific subject areas outlined by the Council. Completion of the 13 modules in *Caring for Preschool Children* enables teachers to meet or exceed the Council's training requirements. (A sample form for documenting contact hours can be found in the Appendix.)

Teachers applying for a Credential are responsible for developing a Professional Resource File, which is a collection of documents to use in working with children and families. The learning activities in *Caring for Preschool Children* include many opportunities for teachers to document work and collect materials for their Professional Resource File.

Direct Assessment also requires teachers to complete a written and oral assessment and to be observed working directly with children. The knowledge and competency assessments that complete each module will help teachers prepare for the CDA assessments.

In the second route to obtaining a CDA Credential, the Council arranges for teachers to enter a college-level Professional Preparation Program, which offers training and assessment using the Council's curriculum, *Essentials*. There are three phases in the CDA Professional Preparation Program: field work, instructional course work, and evaluation.

To keep up-to-date on the process for obtaining a CDA Credential, contact The Council for Professional Recognition at (800) 424-4310 or log on to their Web site (www.cdacouncil.org).

# Using the Modules for Program Improvement

An increasing body of research identifies a link between training, program quality, and positive outcomes for children. The National Child Care Staffing Study suggests that accredited centers provide higher-than-average-quality services. "The accredited centers had better-compensated teachers with more formal education and specialized early childhood training, provided better benefits and working conditions, and maintained lower rates of turnover."[4]

Unfortunately, most state regulations fall far short of ensuring that programs meet standards of quality that all children need to thrive. Welfare reform poses new challenges to the profession as some states consider lowering standards for programs and staff qualifications in order to expand child care services.

One of the benefits of using a comprehensive training program for all staff is that the quality of the program is enhanced as teachers gain new skills and knowledge that they apply to their work. Program accreditation is a voluntary approach for recognizing and promoting high-quality programs serving young children. The accreditation process can be a powerful motivator for everyone working at a site to come together and work toward program improvement.

Accreditation begins with an extensive self-study process focusing on established criteria. All program staff members and parents complete forms to evaluate the program and identify areas where improvement is needed. Many of the trainers and directors who use *Caring for Preschool Children* review the results of this self-assessment process when selecting which modules to introduce to teachers first. For example, if a program does not meet the standards for promoting children's health, all teachers can begin with Module 2, *Healthy*, and discuss each section as a group.

When program staff members think they have met all the criteria, they submit their paperwork to the accrediting organization. This organization arranges a site visit by a validator who verifies the accuracy of the program's self-assessment. The validated self-assessment is reviewed by a commission, or board, that has the power to grant accreditation for a specified period of years, or to defer accreditation and make recommendations on areas that must be improved first. Three national systems now exist for center-based programs.[5]

The National Academy of Early Childhood Programs, a division of NAEYC, administers a national, voluntary, professionally sponsored accreditation system for programs serving children from birth through kindergarten. Since establishing the system in 1985, NAEYC has accredited more than 8100 programs serving approximately three-quarters of a million young children and their families.

**NAEYC National Academy of Early Childhood Programs**
1509 16th Street, N.W.
Washington, DC  20036
(800) 424-2460 or (202) 232-8777
www.naeyc.org

The National Early Childhood Program Accreditation (NECPA) is an independent voluntary accreditation program developed with the National Child Care Association, the largest organization of proprietary child care professionals. Since 1993, the NECPA has accredited 110 centers across the United States.

**The National Early Childhood Program Accreditation Commission**
126C Suber Road
Columbia, SC  29210
800-505-9878
www.necpa.net

National Accreditation Council for Early Childhood Professional Personnel and Programs is a national, non-profit organization that supports private and ecumenical, licensed, center-based early childhood programs. The organization is sponsored by the Child Care Institute of America. Since 1992, the Council has accredited more than 80 programs in various states.

**The National Accreditation Council for Early Childhood Professional Personnel and Programs**
3612 Bent Branch Court
Falls Church, VA  22041
703-941-4329

The chart that follows shows how the modules in *Caring for Preschool Children* might be grouped into a series of courses and how they address the CDA Subject Areas and NAEYC Early Childhood Program Standards. (Note: Beginning in late 2005, programs seeking NAEYC accreditation will have to demonstrate compliance with each of the program standards and criteria developed by the Commission on NAEYC Early Childhood Program Standards and Accreditation Criteria.)

# Using *Caring for Preschool Children* for
# Professional Development and Program Improvement

| Course Title | *Caring for Preschool Children* Modules | Clock Hours | CDA Subject Areas Addressed | NAEYC Early Childhood Program Standards |
|---|---|---|---|---|
| Establishing the Environment | 1-Safe | 12 | Planning a safe, healthy learning environment | Health, Physical Environment |
| | 2-Healthy | 12 | | |
| | 3-Learning Environment | 14 | | |
| Child Growth and Development: Cognitive and Physical | 4-Physical | 10 | Steps to advance children's physical and intellectual development | Curriculum, Relationships, Teaching |
| | 5-Cognitive | 10 | | |
| | 6-Communication | 10 | Principles of child growth and development | |
| | 7-Creative | 10 | | |
| Child Growth and Development: Social and Emotional | 8-Self | 11 | Positive ways to support children's social and emotional development | Curriculum, Relationships, Teaching |
| | 9-Social | 11 | | |
| | 10-Guidance | 16 | Principles of child growth and development | |
| Introduction to the Early Childhood Profession | 11-Families | 10 | Strategies to establish productive relationships with families | Assessment, Teachers, Families, Communities, Leadership, and Management |
| | 12-Program Management | 20 | Strategies to manage an effective program operation | |
| | 13-Professionalism | 10 | Maintaining a commitment to professionalism | |
| | | | Observing and documenting children's behavior | |
| Applied Early Childhood Practices (lab or practicum) | This course would include observations of each student's application of material presented in class and provide individualized support and feedback. | 16 | Observations by an advisor are part of the CDA credentialing process | Site validator visit |

1   National Association for the Education of Young Children. (1993). *A conceptual framework for early childhood professional development*. Washington, DC: Author.

2   The Council for Professional Recognition. (1996). *The child development associate assessment system and competency standards: Preschool caregivers in center-based programs*. Washington, DC: Author.

3   *Op. cit.*

4   Whitebrook, M. (1996). NAEYC accreditation as an indicator of program quality: What research tells us. In S. Bredekamp & B. Willer (Eds.), *NAEYC accreditation: A decade of learning and the years ahead* (p. 35). Washington, DC: National Association for the Education of Young Children.

5   Stoney Associates. (1996). Accreditation as a quality improvement strategy. In *Building and maintaining an effective child care/early education system in your state* (pp. 20-22). Albany, NY: Author.

# Chapter 2

# Supporting the Self-Instructional Training Process

The trainer is central to the success of this self-instructional training program. This chapter suggests ways to introduce the content and format of the training to teachers who will be using the modules. It explains your role in leading teachers through the *Orientation* and the steps of each module and offers suggestions about conducting feedback conferences so they are positive learning experiences.

At the end of this chapter you will find a chart describing what teachers do and what trainers do in each of the 13 modules. For each topic, we also suggest ways to extend learning.

## Introducing the Training Program

In preparing to introduce the training program, make sure you have several copies of *Caring for Preschool Children* that teachers may keep or share and a *Skill-Building Journal* for each teacher to keep. Plan to meet with teachers, individually or in small groups, so you can describe the training content and design and explain how you plan to support, assess, and document their progress.

You might begin by discussing what it means to be a competent teacher and explaining how the modules help teachers expand and build on their knowledge and skills in teaching preschool children. Use the points below.

**Competent teachers apply their knowledge of child development.** They use what they know about preschool children to plan for each child and for the group. The first learning activity in many of the modules summarizes the typical characteristics of preschool children and describes how they are related to the topics addressed in the module. In addition, many learning activities include information about child development and opportunities to apply that knowledge while caring for young children.

**Competent teachers establish strong partnerships with families.** This training program recognizes parents as the prime educators of their children. In addition to completing module 11, *Families*, teachers involve families as they carry out and discuss learning activities in other modules. The modules emphasize the importance of offering a program that corresponds with the ethnicities, cultures, and languages of the children and their families.

**Competent teachers document their systematic, objective observations.** Observations allow teachers to learn about each child, measure children's progress, and evaluate program effectiveness. Information gathered through regular, systematic observations helps teachers learn about each child's needs, skills, interests, and individual characteristics. That information is shared with families and used to plan for the group and for individual children.

**Competent teachers offer a program that meets individual needs.** This topic is addressed in depth in module 12, *Program Management*. In addition, it is reinforced through many learning activities. Teachers observe and report what they learn about individual children. They use what they learn to make decisions about introducing new materials, rearranging the environment, tailoring their interactions, and sharing information with families.

**Competent teachers take time to think about their practices.** Reflection is an important part of most of the learning activities. Teachers plan, implement their ideas, and then report and evaluate what took place. They describe how they might change an activity if they offer it again, what materials they could provide to help a child gain specific skills, what props to offer to enhance children's play, or ways to make the environment safer for children.

## Discuss the Content and Approach

Describe how the modules address the 13 functional areas of the CDA Competencies and support the professional development of preschool teachers. Refer teachers to the description of the 13 functional areas of the CDA Competencies that is provided in the *Orientation* and ask which topics and skills they would most like to learn about and in what order. Point out that *Caring for Preschool Children* can be used flexibly; teachers can begin with whichever module is of most interest.

Invite teachers to think about how they learn best, what helps them gain knowledge and skills. Teachers may mention approaches such as classroom support and feedback by trainers, supervisors, or colleagues; viewing videotapes; reading books or articles; watching someone else perform a task; and discussing an idea or concept. Give specific examples that show how the *Caring for Preschool Children* training approach incorporates these strategies.

## Explain the Importance of Observing and Recording

Explain that teachers will conduct and document observations as they complete many of the learning activities in this training program. If possible, review and help teachers practice the skills used to conduct and record systematic, objective, accurate, and complete observations. As a resource, you can use *Learning Activity A, Collecting Information About Each Child*, in module 12, *Program Management*.

Explain that you, too, will use observation as a tool. You will observe teachers throughout the training program to learn more about their skills and how you can help them continue to grow. Your observation notes will serve as the basis for providing objective feedback to teachers about their progress in applying knowledge and skills and for assessing their competence.

## Describe Your Plan for Feedback Conferences

Describe how the training program is tailored to address individual needs and how it provides a close working relationship between trainer and teacher. Emphasize that, although teachers use the materials independently, they are not left alone to sink or swim. Regular feedback is an integral part of the training process. Describe the purpose and frequency of feedback conferences and the approach (one-on-one, teaching teams, or groups) you plan to use.

If you will be conducting group feedback meetings, explain that these are opportunities for teachers to discuss the learning activities and to support each other. Peer support can encourage teachers as they work with children each day, and it contributes to their professional growth.

Distribute and review the Individual Tracking Form found in the Appendix. Encourage teachers to monitor their own progress. Note the space for the trainer to sign the form when each module is completed.

## Acknowledge Teachers' Accomplishments

The competence teachers gain in their work with children and families as they complete the modules will be rewarding, itself. However, it makes a difference when the program they work for acknowledges their undertaking and completing the training program. If possible, let teachers know the program's plan for offering incentives.

Here are ways that some programs acknowledge and reward teachers' efforts.

- Award increases in salaries and benefits for successfully completing different levels of training.

- Offer a certificate for dinner for two donated by a local restaurant, a new material for the children, or a copy of a favorite resource when a teacher has successfully completed a certain number of modules.

- Show pictures to potential program applicants that highlight individual teachers interacting with children. Write brief summaries of teachers' special interests and accomplishments.

- Hold recognition dinners and award ceremonies for teachers who have completed the program. Invite spouses, parents, and other special guests.

- Offer child care so a teacher and guest can spend an evening out. Teachers might volunteer their child care services to acknowledge a colleague's success.

- Provide special pins, tote bags, or framed certificates that are concrete symbols of a teacher's completion of part or all of the training.

- Post on a bulletin board or include in the program newsletter photographs of teachers who have undertaken or completed the training.

# Completing the *Orientation*

All teachers begin the training program by completing the *Orientation* that describes the value and special features of the training program, provides definitions of the 13 functional areas of the CDA Competencies, and explains the steps in the training process. The *Orientation* ends with a *Self-Assessment*, which lists three major areas of competence related to the topic of each module. Teachers should be encouraged to respond as honestly as possible so they can identify their strengths and interests, as well as areas that need strengthening.

Schedule a time to meet with each teacher to review the *Orientation* and the *Self-Assessment*. Allow enough time (15–30 minutes) to discuss the results and to develop a module-completion plan with the teacher. The plan lists the first three modules to work on, target completion dates, and a tentative schedule for completing the entire training program. Most teachers need about four weeks to complete the sections of a module. The entire training program generally takes 12–18 months to complete.

Try to give teachers substantial autonomy in developing the module-completion plan. Sometimes other factors influence which modules a teacher works on first. For example, the module-completion plan might consider program-wide improvement goals, such as reducing injuries or creating more effective learning environments. In such cases, all teachers would complete the same module so they can work together to achieve the program's goal.

Many trainers, especially those implementing the training program for the first time, find it helpful to have several teachers work on the same module at the same time. This way you can conduct group feedback sessions, and teachers can learn from and provide support to one another. Group sessions also make supervision less time-consuming, but keep in mind that one of the most valuable aspects of the training is the feedback you provide each teacher.

# Completing a Module

Each of the 13 modules follows a consistent format using both *Caring for Preschool Children* and the *Skill-Building Journal*. The chart that follows illustrates how the books are used.

| Section | Caring for Preschool Children | Skill-Building Journal |
|---|---|---|
| **Overview** | An introduction to the topic addressed in the module, identification of three major areas of competence, related strategies, and three brief examples of how teachers apply their knowledge and skills to support children's development and learning. | Questions about each of the examples and sample answers. |
| **Your Own Experiences** | A short discussion of how the topic applies to adults. | A series of questions about personal experiences related to the topic. |
| **Pre-Training Assessment** (presented only in the *Skill-Building Journal*) | | A checklist of how often teachers use key strategies and a question about skills to improve or topics to learn more about. |
| **Learning Activities** (4–5 per module) | Objectives for each *Learning Activity* and several pages of information about the topic. | Instructions for applying the reading to classroom practices. This may involve answering questions; observing children and using the information to address individual needs and interests; completing a checklist; trying new teaching strategies; or planning, implementing, and evaluating a new activity. When appropriate, *Answer Sheets* are provided. |
| **Reflecting on Your Learning** (presented only in the *Skill-Building Journal*) | | An opportunity to consider how the topic relates to curriculum implementation and building partnerships with families. Questions help teachers summarize what they learned. |

Although the content and activities in the modules vary, teachers and trainers follow the same process for completing each one. The process for completing the sections of each module is described in the following paragraphs and illustrated in the diagram on page 23.

## Overview

**Teachers** read about the topic addressed in the module. For each area of competence, they review strategies that teachers use and three examples of how teachers apply their knowledge and skills. Teachers answer questions about each example and compare their answers to those on the *Answer Sheets* in the *Skill-Building Journal* at the end of the module.

## Your Own Experiences

Next, **teachers** answer questions about how the topic relates to their own experiences, both on and off the job. They examine how personal experiences affect their approaches to their work with children and families and their choice of teaching strategies.

## Pre-Training Assessment

**Teachers** complete the *Pre-Training Assessment*—a list of the strategies that competent teachers use—by indicating whether they do these things regularly, sometimes, or not enough. They review their responses and identify 3–5 skills they want to improve or topics they want to learn more about. Teachers can refer to the *Glossary* at the end of *Caring for Preschool Children* for definitions of the terms used.

The **trainer** schedules a time to meet with teachers to discuss the questions about the *Overview*, their own experiences, and the *Pre-Training Assessment*. You might point out what they will be learning and how their skills will be enhanced. **Teachers** then begin the learning activities for the module.

## Learning Activities

Each module includes four or five learning activities. After reading several pages of information about the topic, **teachers** apply their knowledge while working with children and families. For example, they might answer questions related to the reading and their own teaching practices; complete a checklist; try suggestions from the reading and report the results; plan, implement, and evaluate an activity; or observe and record children's behavior and interactions and then use the observation notes to individualize the program. Examples of completed forms, summaries, and charts are provided, when needed, to explain the activity.

The **trainer,** when possible, offers support to teachers as they complete the learning activities. Support might include observing the teacher while he or she works with children, conducting a co-observation of a child, reviewing plans and assisting in collecting materials, or discussing and answering questions about the module content.

The **trainer** schedules a time to meet with teachers, individually or in a group, after they have completed the learning activities. Invite teachers to discuss the content and report what they did and learned. Provide additional feedback based on your observation notes and on the written portion of the learning activity: charts, checklists, plans, responses to questions, or observation summaries. For some activities, teachers meet with colleagues or a child's family, or review *Answer Sheets* at the end of the module.

## Reflecting on Your Learning

After completing all of the learning activities, **teachers** summarize their progress. They review their responses to the *Pre-Training Assessment* and describe their increased knowledge and skills. For some modules, teachers also review and add examples to charts created in one of the learning activities.

**Teachers** meet with their **trainer** to review their progress and to discuss whether they are ready for the knowledge and competency assessments. When teachers are ready, schedule times to administer the *Knowledge Assessment* and conduct the *Competency Assessment* observation. If a teacher needs to learn more about the knowledge and skills addressed in the module, suggest supplemental strategies.

For teachers who are having difficulty mastering the content, or for those who want to learn more about a specific topic, you can suggest other resources. Professional organizations and publishers offer numerous books, journals, videotapes, Web sites, and training manuals related to caring for preschool children. *Caring for Preschool Children* includes a bibliography of resources for early childhood professionals.

## Assessing Knowledge and Competence

There is a *Knowledge Assessment* for each module and a *Competency Assessment* for modules 1-12. Chapter 4 of this *Trainer's Guide, Assessing Each Teacher's Progress*, describes the assessment process and offers guidance on administering, scoring, and discussing the results of the evaluations. It also includes the *Knowledge Assessments, Answer Sheets*, and the *Competency Assessment* observation forms.

## Documenting Progress

After **teachers** have successfully completed the learning activities and both assessments, they can record their progress on the Individual Tracking Form (included in the Appendix) and ask for the trainer's signature. **Trainers** use the Program Tracking Form (in the Appendix) to document and monitor the progress of a group of teachers. Keeping this form up-to-date can help you schedule feedback sessions and assessments.

# The Training Process

**Complete the Orientation**

Read about the training program
Complete the Self-Assessment
Develop a module-completion plan

Feedback
and
Discussion

**Complete a Module**

**Overview**

Read about the topic and three related areas of competence
Review examples of what teachers do
Answer questions

**Your Own Experiences**

Relate topic to own experiences
Answer questions

**Pre-Training Assessment**

Assess own use of strategies
List skills to improve or topics to learn about

**Learning Activities**

Read about topic
Apply knowledge
Answer questions

**Reflecting on Your Learning**

Review responses to Pre-Training Assessment
Summarize skills and knowledge gained
Discuss readiness for assessments

Feedback
and
Discussion

**Not ready for assessment**
Review or repeat activities

**Ready for assessment**
Schedule times

**Assessments**
Knowledge Assessment
Competency Assessment

Feedback
and
Discussion

**Did not demonstrate competence**
Review or repeat activities

**Demonstrated competence**
Document progress
Begin next module

# Providing Feedback

Whether provided one-on-one or during group sessions, your feedback to teachers is central to the success of the training program. Feedback conferences are particularly important because of the self-instructional nature of *Caring for Preschool Children*. These conferences are opportunities for trainers to answer questions, offer support, make suggestions, listen to concerns, reinforce new skills, help teachers recognize how much they have learned, and encourage teachers to repeat activities they may have misunderstood the first time.

For each module, trainers provide feedback after teachers complete

- the *Overview, Your Own Experiences* (with the possible exception of module 3, *Healthy*, if teachers prefer to keep their responses private), and the *Pre-Training Assessment*

- each *Learning Activity*

- *Reflecting on Your Learning*

- the *Knowledge Assessment* and the *Competency Assessment*

Feedback conferences may be as short as 10 minutes or may last longer, depending on how much feedback and support teachers need. Try to schedule a feedback conference for each learning activity before the teacher begins the next one. It is always best to discuss responses that are still fresh in the teacher's mind. A full understanding of each activity is particularly important when a learning activity builds on the knowledge and skills addressed in the previous one.

Encourage teachers to take the initiative in scheduling feedback conferences. You can post a schedule of times when you are available and encourage teachers to sign up when they are ready. When several teachers are working on the same module, a joint decision should be made about when to meet, because everyone will have to be on the same section of the module at the time of the feedback conference.

Here are some suggestions for conducting one-on-one or group feedback sessions. You may adapt them to reflect your own training style and what you know about each teacher.

**Review the written responses to the section before the conference.** This is especially important when preparing to give feedback on inappropriate responses. Consider how to offer constructive comments that encourage teachers to try an activity again.

**Begin with an open-ended question.** For example, you might ask, "What did you think about this activity?" or "What did you learn from this activity?" Take a few minutes to discuss each teacher's response to the question.

**Use specific examples to acknowledge appropriate responses.** For example, "The way you phrased that showed your respect for the child. You told him clearly what you expected, but you were careful to show him you understood his feelings."

**Relate teachers' responses to information in the text.** For example, "Your responses show that you understand how to use the suggested strategies for handling challenging behavior and why they are appropriate."

**Ask questions about inappropriate responses.** Instead of simply correcting them, help teachers think about why responses are inappropriate and how children might be affected. Open-ended questions, such as the following, are helpful:

- What are the reasons for the child's behavior?

- How could you involve the children in this routine?

- What message would this statement send to the child?

**Help teachers arrive at appropriate responses.** You might say, "Let's look at the text. Perhaps there's another way to phrase this so it offers guidance without making the child feel discouraged."

The underlying goal of providing feedback is to improve a teacher's skills and knowledge. If a teacher has not understood the information presented in a section, use the feedback conference to review and explain the information and promote understanding.

# What Teachers and Trainers Do in Each Module

The following charts summarize what teachers and trainers do in each section of the 13 modules. Individual teachers and trainers have different learning and interaction styles. These charts therefore do not present hard-and-fast rules to be followed inflexibly. Rather, they summarize what teachers are asked to do and suggest constructive ways for trainers to provide support. Each chart is followed by suggested strategies for extending learning in individual or group sessions.

# Completing Module 1: Safe

| Module Sections | What Teachers Do | What Trainers Do |
|---|---|---|
| **Overview**<br><br>**Your Own Need for Safety**<br><br>**Pre-Training Assessment** | Read about safety and how teachers keep children safe.<br><br>Read and answer questions about the three examples of how teachers keep children safe and about their own need for safety.<br><br>Complete the *Pre-Training Assessment* and list 3–5 skills to improve or topics to learn more about.<br><br>Share responses and chart feedback. | Observe teachers and review ongoing notes.<br><br>Discuss with teachers:<br><br>• responses to questions about the examples<br><br>• personal safety experiences and how they relate to children's safety<br><br>• the *Pre-Training Assessment*<br><br>When possible, evaluate *Pre-Training Assessment* responses by observing. |
| **Learning Activity A, Creating and Maintaining Safe Environments** | Read about ways teachers promote safety while encouraging children to explore and investigate. Review tips for making indoor interest areas and activities safe.<br><br>Use daily and monthly safety checklists to assess their indoor and outdoor environments, identify items that need attention, and take steps to improve safety.<br><br>Discuss needed improvements with colleagues and trainer. Make and check off changes. With colleagues, develop a schedule for daily and monthly safety checks. Chart feedback. | Review checklists and help teachers identify potential dangers.<br><br>Help teachers plan ways to improve environmental safety.<br><br>Check to ensure that teachers made environmental safety improvements. |
| **Learning Activity B, Keeping Children Safe on Trips Away From the Program** | Read about guidelines for walking safely near traffic with children and for planning safe study trips with children.<br><br>Review program policies and procedures for ensuring children's safety on trips, describe them, and think about improvements that might be needed.<br><br>Describe a child who needs extra support on trips and plan safety precautions.<br><br>Share responses and chart feedback. | Review teachers' descriptions of program policies and discuss identified improvements.<br><br>Discuss teachers' descriptions of children who need extra support on trips and help teachers plan ways to keep children safe. |

## Completing Module 1: Safe (continued)

| Module Sections | What Teachers Do | What Trainers Do |
|---|---|---|
| **Learning Activity C, Handling Injuries and Emergencies** | Read about responding to injuries and emergencies, first-aid procedures, and what to do in case of fire.<br><br>Check the program's first-aid kits and supply any missing items.<br><br>Review program emergency procedures and answer questions about responding to injuries and emergencies.<br><br>If necessary, review program emergency procedures with supervisor.<br><br>Share responses and chart feedback. | Discuss answers to questions.<br><br>Encourage teachers to review and practice emergency procedures on a regular basis.<br><br>Provide additional resources or referrals for additional first-aid and emergency-response training, as needed.<br><br>When possible, observe emergency drills and provide feedback. |
| **Learning Activity D, Helping Children Learn to Take Precautions** | Read about teaching children to keep themselves safe by modeling and explaining safety practices and by helping children predict and avoid unsafe situations.<br><br>Work with a small group of children to develop safety rules for an indoor or outdoor area and answer questions about the process. Create a poster of safety rules to hang in the classroom.<br><br>Share responses and chart feedback. | Help teachers plan a safety discussion with children, if asked.<br><br>If possible, observe teachers conducting safety rule discussions with children and provide feedback.<br><br>Discuss responses to the questions and the teachers' experiences in developing safety rules with children.<br><br>Comment on the posters and children's responses. |
| **Reflecting on Your Learning** | Review responses to the *Pre-Training Assessment*, summarize progress by answering questions, and consider curriculum connections and partnerships with families.<br><br>Share responses and chart feedback.<br><br>Complete the knowledge and competency assessments. | Discuss teachers' progress summaries.<br><br>Give and score the *Knowledge Assessment*.<br><br>Schedule an observation to complete the *Competency Assessment* for this module.<br><br>Provide feedback as teachers work on the assessments. |

### Strategies to Extend Learning

**Have teachers kneel on the floor to view the environment from the children's perspective.** Discuss safety precautions taken (e.g., using electrical outlet covers) as well as any unaddressed hazards teachers discover.

**Distribute information on and encourage teachers to attend safety training courses or workshops.** Consider training offered by the program, by local organizations, or by national groups such as the American Red Cross.

**Ask teachers to individualize safety checklists.** Checklists should correspond to their room arrangements, furnishings, materials, equipment, and outdoor areas.

**Encourage teachers to keep records of how they address potentially dangerous items and conditions.** This exercise will help teachers develop awareness that maintaining a safe environment is an ongoing part of their jobs.

**Suggest that teachers obtain and share safety publications with families.** Consider materials from organizations such as the American Academy of Pediatrics and the Consumer Product Safety Commission.

**Ask local emergency service providers to provide training** on how to respond during weather-related emergencies that might occur in your area (e.g., lightning storms, tornadoes, and earthquakes). The local American Red Cross chapter and fire department can be excellent resources.

# Completing Module 2: Healthy

| Module Sections | What Teachers Do | What Trainers Do |
| --- | --- | --- |
| **Overview**<br><br>**Your Own Health and Nutrition**<br><br>**Pre-Training Assessment** | Read about strategies that promote children's health.<br><br>Read and answer questions about the three examples of how teachers promote children's health and about their own health and nutrition.<br><br>Complete the *Pre-Training Assessment* and list 3–5 skills to improve or topics to learn more about.<br><br>Share responses and chart feedback. | Observe teachers and review ongoing notes.<br><br>Discuss with teachers:<br><br>• responses to questions about the examples<br><br>• personal health habits (if teachers want to share information) and how they relate to children's health<br><br>• the *Pre-Training Assessment*<br><br>When possible, evaluate *Pre-Training Assessment* responses by observing. |
| **Learning Activity A, Creating and Maintaining a Hygienic Environment** | Read about sanitation procedures, including hand washing and disinfecting surfaces, toys, and furniture; hygienic food practices; promoting wellness while children sleep; and maintaining a hygienic bathroom.<br><br>Use a health and hygiene checklist to assess health practices.<br><br>List practices that need improvement and describe improvement strategies.<br><br>Set a date to review the checklist again.<br><br>Share responses and chart feedback. | Review completed checklists and help teachers identify practices that need improvement.<br><br>Meet with teachers and colleagues to discuss improvement strategies that will promote wellness and reduce disease. |
| **Learning Activity B, Responding When Children Are Sick** | Read about the needs of sick children, daily health checks, common childhood diseases, and facts about contagious diseases and lice.<br><br>Read brief stories about children's health and respond to questions on the basis of their program's policies.<br><br>Share responses and chart feedback. | Review teachers' responses to the brief stories. Discuss the implementation of program health and confidentiality policies.<br><br>Suggest resources for teachers to learn more about illnesses and conditions that affect young children.<br><br>Help teachers select and structure cooking activities with children. |

## Completing Module 2: Healthy (continued)

| Module Sections | What Teachers Do | What Trainers Do |
|---|---|---|
| **Learning Activity C, Encouraging Good Nutrition** | Read about the Food Guide Pyramid for Young Children, family-style meals, and cooking with children.<br><br>Plan, conduct, and report on a small-group cooking activity.<br><br>Discuss the cooking activity with the children's families and offer suggestions for cooking with children at home.<br><br>Share responses and chart feedback. | Suggest resources for the cooking activity.<br><br>If possible, observe teachers conducting the food preparation activity.<br><br>Discuss the activity, what children learned, and what changes should be made if the activity is repeated. |
| **Learning Activity D, Helping Children Learn Healthy Habits** | Read about teaching children good health habits through routines, play, and activities.<br><br>Describe a program health routine usually followed without children's involvement. Plan and implement a strategy for including children in the routine. Report what happened and additional changes they might make. Continue adapting routines to include children's active participation.<br><br>Share responses and chart feedback. | Discuss the inclusion of children in health routines.<br><br>Discuss the changes in routines and what teachers and children learned.<br><br>Help teachers examine and make necessary changes to other health routines so that children are actively involved as much as possible. |
| **Learning Activity E, Recognizing and Reporting Child Abuse and Neglect** | Study definitions and signs of different types of child abuse and neglect. Read about clues, possible abuse and neglect in early childhood programs, and reporting issues.<br><br>Answer questions about recognizing and reporting possible child abuse and neglect.<br><br>Read reasons why teachers might be reluctant to respond to signs of possible neglect and abuse and explain why they must respond.<br><br>Review their program's procedures and state and local procedures for reporting abuse and neglect. Answer questions about the procedures.<br><br>Share responses and chart feedback. | Provide definitions of and guidance on child abuse and neglect. Present information from the program and from state and local governments.<br><br>Review answers to the questions and help teachers compare them to those provided in the *Answer Sheets*. |

## Completing Module 2: Healthy (continued)

| Module Sections | What Teachers Do | What Trainers Do |
|---|---|---|
| **Reflecting on Your Learning** | Review responses to the *Pre-Training Assessment*, summarize progress by answering questions, and consider curriculum connections and partnerships with families.<br><br>Share responses and chart feedback.<br><br>Complete the knowledge and competency assessments. | Discuss teachers' progress summaries.<br><br>Give and score the *Knowledge Assessment*.<br><br>Schedule an observation to complete the *Competency Assessment* for this module.<br><br>Provide feedback as teachers work on the assessments. |

### Strategies to Extend Learning

**Ask teachers to review and discuss their programs' menus for snacks and meals.** Recommend changes, if necessary, to ensure that foods served to children meet USDA guidelines.

**Encourage teachers to ask families to share their favorite recipes.** Provide materials and help teachers create picture recipe cards.

**Maintain and share with teachers a file of recipes and plans for simple cooking activities.** Encourage teachers to maintain their own files. Suggest that they take photographs of children involved in cooking activities and share them with families and colleagues.

**Serve healthy snacks at staff meetings and workshops.** Discuss ways teachers model good nutrition and hygiene practices, such as healthy eating habits and washing their hands before eating.

**Ask teachers to help you organize a collection of local resources on the prevention of child abuse and neglect.** Work together to plan and implement family support activities at the program.

**Visit a program at meal or snack time.** Model strategies for relaxed, family-style dining, before, during, and after eating.

**Encourage teachers to meet regularly to discuss stresses that may affect children and families and to suggest strategies for offering assistance.** Ask teachers to share their healthy approaches to stress, and encourage them to support each other on the job.

# Completing Module 3: Learning Environment

| Module Sections | What Teachers Do | What Trainers Do |
|---|---|---|
| **Overview**<br><br>**Your Own Responses to the Environment**<br><br>**Pre-Training Assessment** | Read about the importance of creating effective indoor and outdoor learning environments and about schedules, routines, and transitions that support children's learning.<br><br>Read and answer questions about the three examples of how teachers create and use learning environments for preschool children and about personal responses to the environment.<br><br>Complete the *Pre-Training Assessment* and list 3–5 skills to improve or topics to learn more about.<br><br>Share responses and chart feedback. | Observe teachers and learning environments and review ongoing notes.<br><br>Discuss with teachers:<br><br>• responses to questions about the examples<br><br>• personal experiences in different environments and how they relate to creating appropriate learning environments for children<br><br>• the *Pre-Training Assessment*<br><br>When possible, evaluate *Pre-Training Assessment* responses by observing. |
| **Learning Activity A, Using Your Knowledge of Child Development to Create a Learning Environment** | Read about typical behaviors of preschool children and how carefully planned environments support their learning.<br><br>Complete the chart showing how teachers use their knowledge of child development to create supportive learning environments.<br><br>Share responses and chart feedback.<br><br>Continue adding examples to the chart while working on the module. | Discuss how teachers create environments that correspond to and support children's development.<br><br>Discuss examples that teachers recorded on their charts.<br><br>Share your observations of how the environments the teachers have created promote children's learning.<br><br>Encourage teachers to add examples to the chart while working on the module. |
| **Learning Activity B, Setting Up and Maintaining Classroom Interest Areas** | Read about the creation of interest areas and the selection and display of materials.<br><br>Identify and compare the strengths and weaknesses of two classroom arrangements.<br><br>Draw a floor plan of their classrooms and describe the changes they want to make to improve the learning environment.<br><br>Identify items they now have in each interest area and assess the organization and display of materials and equipment.<br><br>List the changes they want to make in one interest area, how the changes might help, and children's reactions to changes.<br><br>Share responses and chart feedback. | Help teachers identify and compare the strengths and weaknesses of the example floor plans and of the teachers' floor plans.<br><br>Discuss plans to improve the indoor and outdoor environments. If possible, meet with teachers and their colleagues to review proposed changes and encourage teamwork. Help teachers rearrange their environments according to their plans.<br><br>Encourage teachers regularly to observe children's responses to the environment and to determine when additional changes are needed. |

## Completing Module 3: Learning Environment (continued)

| Module Sections | What Teachers Do | What Trainers Do |
|---|---|---|
| **Learning Activity C, Organizing the Outdoor Environment** | Read about the characteristics of outdoor environments that offer children a range of experiences, adapting the environment for children with disabilities, and how children use different materials and equipment. Determine what materials and equipment are needed to improve their programs' outdoor environments.<br><br>Identify current outdoor activities.<br><br>Develop and implement plans to add or improve three activities, and record what children do.<br><br>Share responses and chart feedback. | Help teachers understand the arrangement of effective outdoor learning environments. Review and discuss plans. Ask teachers to explain how the plans will help give children new experiences.<br><br>If appropriate, help teachers obtain or make new items.<br><br>Discuss children's reactions to the changes. |
| **Learning Activity D, Planning the Daily Schedule and Routines** | Read about appropriate daily schedules, routines, and transition times.<br><br>Assess their current daily schedules and identify needed changes.<br><br>Determine a new approach for one routine or transition. Implement and evaluate the plan.<br><br>Share responses and chart feedback. | Discuss the effectiveness of daily schedules and plans for carrying out routines and transitions.<br><br>If possible, observe routines and transitions.<br><br>Help teachers identify strengths and problems and propose solutions. |
| **Reflecting on Your Learning** | Review responses to the *Pre-Training Assessment*, add to the child development chart, summarize progress by answering questions, and consider curriculum connections and partnerships with families.<br><br>Share responses and chart feedback.<br><br>Complete the knowledge and competency assessments. | Discuss teachers' additions to their child development charts and their progress summaries.<br><br>Give and score the *Knowledge Assessment*.<br><br>Schedule an observation to complete the *Competency Assessment* for this module.<br><br>Provide feedback as teachers work on the assessments. |

**Strategies to Extend Learning**

Show the *Room Arrangement as a Teaching Strategy* video. Discuss what teachers want to do in order to convey the positive messages discussed in the video.

Provide materials for making classroom labels and help teachers organize and label materials in their classrooms. Use materials such as clear and solid colors of adhesive paper, poster board, construction paper, permanent markers, and glue.

Suggest that teachers plan and hold a workshop for families on learning environments at the center and at home. Discuss topics such as

- messages in the environment

- how the environment promotes active learning

- how children learn to take care of materials and equipment

Help teachers set up a system for collecting and storing useful materials. Teachers can use cardboard boxes and plastic containers to store dramatic play props, paper, and art materials.

# Completing Module 4: Physical

| Module Sections | What Teachers Do | What Trainers Do |
|---|---|---|
| **Overview**<br><br>**Taking Care of Your Body**<br><br>**Pre-Training Assessment** | Read about fine and gross motor development and what teachers do to promote preschool children's physical development.<br><br>Read and answer questions about the three examples of how teachers promote children's physical development and about staying physically fit, themselves.<br><br>Complete the *Pre-Training Assessment* and list 3–5 skills to improve or topics to learn more about.<br><br>Share responses and chart feedback. | Observe teachers and review ongoing notes.<br><br>Discuss with teachers:<br><br>• responses to questions about the examples<br><br>• ways to handle the physical demands of their jobs<br><br>• the *Pre-Training Assessment*<br><br>When possible, evaluate *Pre-Training Assessment* responses by observing. |
| **Learning Activity A, Using Your Knowledge of Child Development to Promote Physical Development** | Read about preschool children's typical physical development, how physical development is connected to other aspects of development, and physical development alerts.<br><br>Complete the chart showing how teachers use their knowledge of child development to promote children's fine and gross motor skills.<br><br>Share responses and chart feedback.<br><br>Continue adding examples to the chart while working on the module. | Discuss what teachers do to encourage children to develop and use gross and fine motor skills.<br><br>Review examples that teachers recorded on their charts.<br><br>Share your observations of how teachers are supporting children's use of fine and gross motor skills.<br><br>Encourage teachers to add examples to the chart while working on the module. |
| **Learning Activity B, Creating an Environment That Supports Physical Development** | Read about materials and equipment that help children develop their fine and gross motor skills.<br><br>Complete a chart identifying the equipment and materials they provide in each interest area and outdoors, how children use their physical skills, and what they might add to further promote children's physical development.<br><br>Conduct frequent assessments of the environment and make changes as necessary.<br><br>Share responses and chart feedback. | Review and discuss how activities in each interest area encourage children to develop and refine physical skills.<br><br>Ask teachers to explain how the materials they might add would promote motor skill development.<br><br>If appropriate, suggest equipment and materials. |

## Completing Module 4: Physical (continued)

| Module Sections | What Teachers Do | What Trainers Do |
|---|---|---|
| **Learning Activity C, Observing and Responding to Children's Growing Physical Skills** | Read about the continuum of fine and gross motor development and how teachers use their knowledge to plan.<br><br>Observe and record examples of at least two fine and two gross motor skills that a child uses over a 5-day period.<br><br>Identify the child's developmental level for each skill, how they responded to the child's action, and an activity to help the child practice and refine each skill.<br><br>Share responses and chart feedback. | Discuss observation summaries: the examples teachers recorded, the level teachers identified for each skill, how they responded, the children's reactions, and the activities teachers planned.<br><br>Suggest materials, routines, and activities that give children opportunities to practice and refine gross and fine motor skills. |
| **Learning Activity D, Promoting Children's Gross Motor Skills** | Read about offering cues and challenges to help children use and refine their gross motor skills.<br><br>Identify children who will benefit from cues or challenges. Prepare and implement an activity plan that incorporates cues and challenges. Record what happened and what changes they will make if they offer the activity again.<br><br>Share responses and chart feedback. | Review activity plans and give suggestions for observing children and offering appropriate cues and challenges.<br><br>Discuss activity experiences and what teachers learned about promoting physical development. |
| **Reflecting on Your Learning** | Review responses to the *Pre-Training Assessment*, add examples to the child development chart, summarize progress by answering questions, and consider curriculum connections and partnerships with families.<br><br>Share responses and chart feedback.<br><br>Complete the knowledge and competency assessments | Discuss teachers' additions to their physical development charts and their progress summaries.<br><br>Give and score the *Knowledge Assessment*.<br><br>Schedule an observation to complete the *Competency Assessment* for this module.<br><br>Provide feedback as teachers work on the assessments. |

### Strategies to Extend Learning

**Observe children who seem to have unusual delays in fine or gross motor skill development.** Share your observation notes with teachers and, if needed, with the children's families. Encourage families to follow up with their pediatrician or a specialist, if necessary.

**Hold a workshop during which teachers use their fine motor skills** for woodworking, finger painting, cooking, completing puzzles, setting the table, building with Legos, stringing beads, water play, and outdoor mural painting. Point out the small muscle skills developed through these and similar activities.

**Lead role playing for teachers to practice encouraging children who are developing physical skills.** Teachers can practice offering cues and challenges to help children develop and refine their skills. Ask two teachers to pretend that they are children engaged in an activity, while a third teacher provides encouragement, cues, and challenges. Switch roles so everyone has a turn playing a child and the teacher. Discuss how it feels to give and receive encouragement.

**Ask teachers to show their colleagues how to play a non-competitive game or conduct an activity that encourages physical fitness.** Provide blank forms so teachers can describe the game or activity, list the materials and equipment, present guidelines, and suggest variations so children with a wide range of physical skills can participate.

# Completing Module 5: Cognitive

| Module Sections | What Teachers Do | What Trainers Do |
| --- | --- | --- |
| **Overview**<br><br>**Your Own Experiences With Learning**<br><br>**Pre-Training Assessment** | Read about cognitive development and how teachers promote preschool children's thinking skills.<br><br>Read and answer questions about the three examples of how teachers promote children's cognitive development and about a personal learning experience.<br><br>Complete the *Pre-Training Assessment* and list 3–5 skills to improve or topics to learn more about.<br><br>Share responses and chart feedback. | Observe teachers and review ongoing notes.<br><br>Discuss with teachers:<br><br>• responses to questions about the examples<br><br>• teachers' personal learning experiences and how those experiences apply to teaching young children<br><br>• the *Pre-Training Assessment*<br><br>When possible, evaluate *Pre-Training Assessment* responses by observing. |
| **Learning Activity A, Using Your Knowledge of Child Development to Promote Cognitive Development** | Read about how preschool children think and learn, and how cognitive development is connected to other aspects of development.<br><br>Complete the chart showing how teachers use their knowledge of child development to promote children's cognitive development.<br><br>Share responses and chart feedback.<br><br>Continue adding examples to the chart while working on the module. | Discuss what teachers do to promote children's cognitive development.<br><br>Review examples that teachers recorded on their charts.<br><br>Share observations of how teachers are supporting children's thinking and problem-solving skills.<br><br>Encourage teachers to add examples to the chart while working on the module. |
| **Learning Activity B, Encouraging Children to Explore and Investigate** | Read about how children use a variety of skills to explore the world and make discoveries, the purposes of teachers' questions, and how open-ended questions help children build on what they already know.<br><br>Describe three situations where they asked children open-ended questions and record what happened.<br><br>Observe and note two situations where children encountered a problem and teachers helped the children construct a way to approach it.<br><br>Share responses and chart feedback. | Review teachers' open-ended questions and the children's responses.<br><br>Discuss the teachers' observations and how they helped children construct understandings. |

# Completing Module 5: Cognitive (continued)

| Module Sections | What Teachers Do | What Trainers Do |
|---|---|---|
| **Learning Activity C, Helping Children Learn About Mathematics** | Read about five areas of mathematics, skills preschool children can learn, and how to provide opportunities for children to use mathematical thinking every day.<br><br>Describe occasions when they engaged children in exploring each of the five mathematical concepts and what happened.<br><br>Share responses and chart feedback. | Discuss the examples teachers describe and clarify any misunderstandings about the development of mathematical thinking.<br><br>Suggest learning experiences teachers can provide every day to promote children's mathematical thinking. |
| **Learning Activity D, Engaging Children in a Study** | Read about selecting an appropriate topic for children to study, making a web of the topic to identify what children can learn, finding out what children already know, ways to explore the topic, involving children in the investigation, and concluding the study.<br><br>Identify a topic and develop a plan for a study, including a web of the topic, the investigative experiences they will offer children, how children will represent what they are learning, and how they will conclude the study.<br><br>Share responses and chart feedback. | Discuss study topics and plans. Suggest materials, resources, and learning experiences, if appropriate. Offer to help teachers implement their plans.<br><br>When possible, observe children's involvement in the investigation.<br><br>Help teachers focus their observations of children engaged in the study, so the teachers will know what materials and experiences to offer in response to children's changing skills and interests. |
| **Reflecting on Your Learning** | Review responses to the *Pre-Training Assessment*, add examples to the child development chart, summarize progress by answering questions, and consider curriculum connections and partnerships with families.<br><br>Share responses and chart feedback.<br><br>Complete the knowledge and competency assessments. | Discuss teacher's additions to their cognitive development charts and their progress summaries.<br><br>Give and score the *Knowledge Assessment*.<br><br>Schedule an observation to complete the *Competency Assessment* for this module.<br><br>Provide feedback as teachers work on the assessments. |

**Strategies to Extend Learning**

**Suggest posting a list of open-ended questions in the classroom.** Teachers can use this list as a reminder (*e.g., What did you find out? What do you notice? How many ways could you...?*).

**Hold a workshop on the five areas of mathematics.** Teachers will gain a deeper understanding of the areas and share ideas about how to provide opportunities each day for children to think mathematically.

**In visits to classrooms, point out opportunities for extending children's learning.** Share examples of how children are constructing understanding as they explore and investigate.

**Identify appropriate topics for long-term studies.** Work with teachers to introduce these topics to children to see whether they are interested in learning more about them.

# Completing Module 6: Communication

| Module Sections | What Teachers Do | What Trainers Do |
|---|---|---|
| **Overview**<br><br>**Your Own Experiences With Communication**<br><br>**Pre-Training Assessment** | Read about communication and language skills and what teachers do to promote children's communication skills.<br><br>Read and respond to questions about the three examples of how teachers promote children's communication skills and about personal communication skills.<br><br>Complete the *Pre-Training Assessment* and list 3–5 skills to improve or topics to learn more about.<br><br>Share responses and chart feedback. | Observe teachers and review ongoing notes.<br><br>Discuss with teachers:<br><br>• responses to questions about the examples<br><br>• teachers' memories of learning language and how those experiences relate to promoting children's communication skills<br><br>• the *Pre-Training Assessment*<br><br>When possible, evaluate *Pre-Training Assessment* responses by observing. |
| **Learning Activity A, Using Your Knowledge of Child Development to Support Language Development** | Read about how preschool children develop language and literacy skills, typical developmental characteristics that are related to language development, how language development is connected to other aspects of development, and communication development alerts.<br><br>Complete the chart showing how teachers use their knowledge of child development to promote children's language skills.<br><br>Share responses and chart feedback.<br><br>Continue adding examples to the chart while working on the module. | Discuss what teachers do to help children develop and use language skills.<br><br>Review the examples teachers recorded on their charts.<br><br>Share observations of how teachers help children use language in different ways and for different purposes.<br><br>Encourage teachers to add examples to the chart while working on the module. |
| **Learning Activity B, Creating a Literacy-Rich Environment** | Read about learning environments that promote literacy and helping families provide literacy-rich homes.<br><br>Observe a child involved in literacy activities and complete the Early Literacy Skills Summary. Describe their classroom environment, new ways to support early literacy skills, and how children respond.<br><br>Share responses and chart feedback. | If possible, observe the same child using literacy skills.<br><br>Suggest ways to make changes to enrich language and literacy environments. |

## Completing Module 6: Communication (continued)

| Module Sections | What Teachers Do | What Trainers Do |
|---|---|---|
| **Learning Activity C, Encouraging Children to Listen and Speak** | Read about environments that support oral communication, helping children learn the rules of conversation and expand their understanding and vocabularies, and supporting English language learners.<br><br>Observe two children's use of language and plan strategies and activities to encourage their listening and speaking. Try the strategies and activities for two weeks and report results.<br><br>Share responses and chart feedback. | Review teachers' observation notes and the plans for using specific strategies and activities to encourage listening and speaking. Offer feedback and suggestions.<br><br>Discuss what happened during the two-week period and how teachers can continue encouraging all children to listen and speak. |
| **Learning Activity D, Reading Aloud and Talking About Books** | Read about the importance of reading aloud with children, choosing appropriate books, and strategies for reading aloud.<br><br>Select two books that are appropriate for the children in the classroom. Read one to a small group and one to an individual child. Report each experience.<br><br>Share responses and chart feedback. | Encourage teachers to assess their book displays regularly to make sure the current selections correspond with children's skills, interests, experiences, and characteristics.<br><br>Discuss reports on reading to small groups and individuals. Help teachers compare the two experiences and discuss strategies for engaging children with books.<br><br>Suggest that teachers keep track of when they read to individuals, to make sure every child has regular one-on-one reading experiences. |
| **Reflecting on Your Learning** | Review responses to the *Pre-Training Assessment*, add examples to the child development chart, summarize progress by answering questions, and consider curriculum connections and partnerships with families.<br><br>Share responses and chart feedback.<br><br>Complete the knowledge and competency assessments. | Discuss teacher's additions to their communication development charts and their progress summaries.<br><br>Give and score the *Knowledge Assessment*.<br><br>Schedule an observation to complete the *Competency Assessment* for the module.<br><br>Provide feedback as teachers work on the assessments. |

### Strategies to Extend Learning

**Ask teachers if you may audio- or videotape their conversations with children, and review the tape together.** Discuss ways teachers encourage children's listening and speaking skills and what they can do to enhance their practice.

**Invite a speech and language specialist to co-lead a workshop on signs of possible speech or language delays or disabilities.** Work with the program director to establish a system for informing families of teachers' observations and making referrals to speech and language specialists, if necessary.

**During classroom visits, model effective oral reading techniques.** Begin by reading to children, individually or in small groups.

**Invite a children's librarian to visit the program to share information** about books and library services for preschool children and families.

**Work with teachers to plan a family workshop on creating home literacy environments that encourage children to explore reading and writing.** Share materials families can use to establish portable reading and writing centers in their homes.

**Collect literacy-related materials in English and children's home languages.** These might include clean, empty food containers; signs; travel posters; calendars; magazines; phone books; and message pads. Have teachers share ideas about organizing and displaying materials to encourage children to explore literacy while they play. Ask them to make a flyer to send home with children explaining the use of simple inexpensive items to support language and literacy learning.

## Completing Module 7: Creative

| Module Sections | What Teachers Do | What Trainers Do |
|---|---|---|
| **Overview**<br><br>**Your Own Creativity**<br><br>**Pre-Training Assessment** | Read about how children express themselves creatively and ways teachers support them.<br><br>Read and answer questions about the three examples of how teachers encourage children's creativity and about adult creativity.<br><br>Complete the *Pre-Training Assessment* and list 3–5 skills to improve or topics to learn more about.<br><br>Share responses and chart feedback. | Observe teachers and review ongoing notes.<br><br>Discuss with teachers:<br><br>• responses to questions about the examples<br><br>• teachers' exploration of open-ended materials<br><br>• the *Pre-Training Assessment*<br><br>When possible, evaluate *Pre-Training Assessment* responses by observing. |
| **Learning Activity A, Using Your Knowledge of Child Development to Encourage Creativity** | Read about key characteristics and typical behavior of preschool children that are related to creativity.<br><br>Create a poster illustrating the characteristics of children that are related to creativity, and keep a log of when children show these characteristics.<br><br>Share responses and chart feedback. | Share observations of how teachers promote children's creativity.<br><br>Review and discuss the examples teachers recorded on their logs.<br><br>Suggest additional ways teachers' interactions can support children's creativity. |
| **Learning Activity B, Supporting Creativity Throughout the Day** | Read about materials and activities that encourage children's creativity in all interest areas and about how teachers' interactions and open-ended questions encourage creativity and let children know their ideas are valued.<br><br>Rate how well their environments and teaching practices support children's creativity throughout the day and identify any needed changes.<br><br>Share responses and chart feedback. | Review teachers' examples and ratings and offer feedback.<br><br>Observe teachers and discuss specific examples of how their interactions with children encourage creativity. |

# Completing Module 7: Creative (continued)

| Module Sections | What Teachers Do | What Trainers Do |
|---|---|---|
| **Learning Activity C, Encouraging Self-Expression Though Music and Movement** | Read about providing opportunities for children to listen to different sounds and music, singing with children, playing rhythm instruments, and encouraging creative movement.<br><br>Answer questions about ways their current music and movement activities encourage self-expression and a way to improve each. Select and implement a new idea and explain what happened.<br><br>Share responses and chart feedback. | Review and discuss the music and movement activities teachers listed, the improvement strategies they implemented, and their reports of what happened.<br><br>Encourage teachers to work with colleagues to implement other new ideas for encouraging self-expression through music and movement. |
| **Learning Activity D, Offering Art Experiences That Invite Exploration and Experimentation** | Read about why children enjoy the process of using art materials; open-ended art activities; developmental stages of drawing and painting; paints, painting tools, and paper; collages and structures; and playdough and clay. Review a chart of suggested art materials.<br><br>Observe a child engaged with art over a 3-day period. Use what they learn about the child to select, plan, and implement a new art activity to match the child's interests and skill level. Report what happened.<br><br>Share responses and chart feedback. | Help teachers plan ways to provide a variety of open-ended art materials and experiences that allow children fully to explore creative processes.<br><br>Review and discuss observation notes and activity plans.<br><br>If possible, observe teachers implementing the activities.<br><br>Assist in cleaning up after messy activities. Model ways to include children in cleanup: sweeping, mopping, wiping tables, and so on. |
| **Reflecting on Your Learning** | Review the log that was started in *Learning Activity A* and add more examples of children's creativity.<br><br>Review responses to the *Pre-Training Assessment*, summarize progress by answering questions, and consider curriculum connections and partnerships with families.<br><br>Share responses and chart feedback.<br><br>Complete the knowledge and competency assessments. | Discuss teachers' additions to their logs and their progress summaries.<br><br>Give and score the *Knowledge Assessment*.<br><br>Schedule an observation to complete the *Competency Assessment* for this module.<br><br>Provide feedback as teachers work on the assessments. |

### Strategies to Extend Learning

**Offer a hands-on, open-ended workshop on the creative process.** (For ideas, see *Learning to Play Again: A Constructivist Workshop for Adults* at http://www.naeyc.org/resources/journal/2003/ConstructWorkshops_Chalufour.pdf). Provide a wide variety of materials and encourage teachers to become fully involved. Help teachers focus on the process rather than the products of their creative work. At the end of the workshop, ask participants to discuss their feelings about focusing on the creative process. Discuss how their experiences will affect their approach to encouraging children's creativity.

**Encourage teachers to identify what they really love to do and plan ways to explore their creativity in those areas.** Have them think of ways to include their interests in their work with children.

**Ask teachers to recall a time during their childhood when an adult supported their creativity.** Guide them by asking questions such as, *What were you doing? What did the adult do and say? How did you feel?* Ask them to list the strategies adults used to encourage them. Next, ask teachers to think of a time when an adult prevented them from being creative. List the adult behavior that interfered with their creativity. Use the two lists to discuss how teachers actively encourage children's creative efforts.

**Have teachers set up a system for keeping examples of children's creativity in individual portfolios.** Each portfolio can include paintings and drawings, photographs of block structures or playdough creations, audiotaped music, descriptions of dances and movement activities, and so on. Both teachers and parents can write brief notes describing children's use of creative thinking and problem-solving skills. Remind teachers to review the portfolios periodically, revisit them with children, and share them with families.

# Completing Module 8: Self

| Module Sections | What Teachers Do | What Trainers Do |
| --- | --- | --- |
| **Overview**<br><br>**Your Own Sense of Self**<br><br>**Pre-Training Assessment** | Read about how children develop a sense of self and the important roles that teachers and families play.<br><br>Read and answer questions about the three examples of how teachers foster children's sense of competence and self-esteem, and about their own experiences.<br><br>Complete the *Pre-Training Assessment* and list 3–5 skills to improve or topics to learn more about.<br><br>Share responses and chart feedback. | Observe teachers and review ongoing notes.<br><br>Discuss with teachers:<br><br>• responses to questions about the examples<br><br>• experiences that contributed to their values, expectations, and sense of identity and how their sense of self influences their relationships with children<br><br>• the *Pre-Training Assessment*<br><br>When possible, evaluate *Pre-Training Assessment* responses by observing. |
| **Learning Activity A, Using Your Knowledge of Child Development to Help Children Build a Sense of Self** | Read about the stages of social/emotional development, the typical developmental characteristics of preschool children that are related to building a sense of self, and the ways in which building a sense of self is connected to all aspects of development.<br><br>Complete the chart showing how teachers use their knowledge of child development to foster children's positive sense of self.<br><br>Share responses and chart feedback.<br><br>Continue adding examples to the chart while working on the module. | Discuss what teachers do to help children learn about themselves and others and develop a positive sense of self.<br><br>Review examples that teachers record on their charts.<br><br>Share your observations of how teachers help children build a sense of self.<br><br>Encourage teachers to add examples to the chart while working on the module. |
| **Learning Activity B, Appreciating Each Child as an Individual** | Read about strategies for getting to know individual children; for understanding what makes each child unique; and for planning a program that accommodates children's varied skills, abilities, and interests.<br><br>Observe two children involved in activities and conversations. Use notes to describe each child and plan ways to help each continue to learn about him- or herself.<br><br>Share responses and chart feedback. | If possible, observe the same children whom teachers observed.<br><br>Discuss the teachers' descriptions of children and their plans for encouraging children to continue self-discovery.<br><br>Encourage teachers to work with colleagues to create a system for conducting regular observations of children and to continually evaluate their interactions with children. |

## Completing Module 8: Self (continued)

| Module Sections | What Teachers Do | What Trainers Do |
|---|---|---|
| **Learning Activity C, Offering a Program That Promotes Success** | Read about planning activities and creating environments that match children's interests and abilities and provide them with challenges to encourage continual growth and learning.<br><br>Observe the same two children as in *Learning Activity B*. Use notes to plan ways to promote each child's success through interactions, the environment, activities, and routines.<br><br>Share responses and chart feedback. | Review charts and teachers' plans.<br><br>Help teachers assess interactions, the environment, activities, and routines to determine how well these are contributing to children's positive sense of self.<br><br>Emphasize that it is important to observe children regularly because children's abilities and interests change frequently. |
| **Learning Activity D, Using Language That Conveys Respect for Children and Their Feelings** | Read about the importance of showing respect for children by listening carefully to them and using positive and supportive language.<br><br>Write examples of what a teacher might say to respond to children in a variety of typical situations.<br><br>Audio- or videotape their conversations with children, evaluate the effectiveness of their language, and think about ways to improve their communication with children.<br><br>Share responses and chart feedback. | Acknowledge teachers' use of caring language. Provide encouragement and feedback as they interact positively with children.<br><br>Model respectful ways of speaking and listening to children.<br><br>Discuss teachers' examples of responses to children in typical situations. If necessary, help teachers rephrase them in positive terms.<br><br>If teachers agree, tape their conversations with children and discuss the effectiveness of their language. |
| **Reflecting on Your Learning** | Review responses to the *Pre-Training Assessment*, add to the child development chart, summarize progress by answering questions, and consider curriculum connections and partnerships with families.<br><br>Share responses and chart feedback.<br><br>Complete the knowledge and competency assessments. | Discuss teacher's additions to their child development charts and their progress summaries.<br><br>Give and score the *Knowledge Assessment*.<br><br>Schedule an observation to complete the *Competency Assessment* for the module.<br><br>Provide feedback as teachers work on the assessments. |

### Strategies to Extend Learning

**Ask teachers to suggest new materials that offer greater challenges.** Consider materials that allow children to use skills they are not currently using; provide greater variety; and correspond to children's families, ethnicities, cultures, home languages, and personal characteristics. Help teachers collect items to help children construct understandings about themselves and others, such as dramatic play props, and help set priorities for purchasing others.

**Encourage teachers to keep families up-to-date about their children's skills, interests, and accomplishments.** Have teachers role-play conversations with families about different ways to promote children's sense of competence through simple routines and activities at home.

**Have teachers think about people they especially enjoyed being with when they were children.** Ask them to picture themselves talking with one of those people. Ask questions, such as the following, to discuss how adults help children recognize their abilities and feel competent.

> *What did this person do or say to help you feel good about yourself?*
>
> *How did you feel about yourself at the time?*
>
> *How did your experiences with this person affect your sense of competence?*
>
> *What can you do and say to help children feel confident about their abilities?*

**Lead a discussion about program routines: what teachers do and how they involve children.** Make a list of daily classroom tasks; then separate it into three categories: tasks children can do alone, tasks children can do with some guidance from teachers, and tasks that teachers or other staff must take care of for health or safety reasons. List materials and equipment, such as small pitchers and brooms, that allow children to do meaningful jobs. Assess whether classroom arrangements encourage children's independence. For example, are toys, materials, and items such as tissues and paper towels stored within children's reach? Do children have easy access to the materials and equipment they need to carry out their plans?

# Completing Module 9: Social

| Module Sections | What Teachers Do | What Trainers Do |
|---|---|---|
| **Overview**<br><br>**Your Own Social Development**<br><br>**Pre-Training Assessment** | Read about the importance of social development, how children develop social skills, and what teachers do to promote children's social skills.<br><br>Read and respond to questions about the three examples of how teachers promote children's social skills and about adult social skills.<br><br>Complete the *Pre-Training Assessment* and list 3–5 skills to improve or topics to learn more about.<br><br>Share responses and chart feedback. | Observe teachers and review ongoing notes.<br><br>Discuss with teachers:<br><br>• responses to questions about the examples<br><br>• how children learn from teachers and how teachers model social skills<br><br>• the *Pre-Training Assessment*<br><br>When possible, evaluate *Pre-Training Assessment* responses by observing. |
| **Learning Activity A, Using Your Knowledge of Child Development to Promote Social Development** | Read about how children use social skills, typical characteristics of preschool children related to social development, how social development is connected to other aspects of development, and social development alerts.<br><br>Complete the chart showing how teachers use their knowledge of child development to promote social development.<br><br>Share responses and chart feedback.<br><br>Continue adding examples to the chart while working on the module. | Discuss strategies to help children develop and use social skills.<br><br>Review the examples teachers recorded on their charts.<br><br>Share your observations of children using social skills in their play.<br><br>Encourage teachers to add examples to their charts while working on the module. |
| **Learning Activity B, Offering a Program That Supports Social Development** | Read about how the physical environment and the program support children's social development.<br><br>Select a program practice and describe how it affects social development. Plan improvements in program practices, implement changes, and report what happened.<br><br>Share responses and chart feedback. | Discuss program features that support social development. Ask teachers to give examples of how their practices support social development.<br><br>Review and offer feedback on plans and reports.<br><br>If possible, observe in classrooms and offer appropriate suggestions. |

# Completing Module 9: Social (continued)

| Module Sections | What Teachers Do | What Trainers Do |
|---|---|---|
| **Learning Activity C, Supporting Children's Dramatic Play** | Read about four kinds of children's play, environments that support dramatic play, and what teachers do to guide and extend children's play.<br><br>Create a prop box, observe children using the props, describe the children's play and social skills, and develop and implement a plan for extending their play.<br><br>Share responses and chart feedback. | Offer to help collect items for prop boxes. Suggest props that correspond to the children's cultures, ethnicities, families, and home languages.<br><br>Discuss teachers' observations and plans for extending play. Help teachers think of props to add to the box and other ways to guide children's play. |
| **Learning Activity D, Helping Children Learn Caring Behavior** | Read about recognizing and encouraging children's caring behavior.<br><br>Conduct 5-minute observations, several times a day, for three days. Review notes and list examples of children's caring behavior.<br><br>Think about their behavior and interactions. Note examples of when they model caring behavior.<br><br>Make and read a book to children about caring behavior. Describe children's responses.<br><br>Share responses and chart feedback. | Review observation summaries and discuss ways to further encourage caring behaviors.<br><br>Share observations of how teachers encourage children's caring behavior.<br><br>Discuss the books and reading experiences. Encourage teachers to continue making books about the children in their care. |
| **Learning Activity E, Helping Children to Make Friends** | Read about the role of teachers in helping children make friends, interact positively, and solve social problems, especially children who are shy, aggressive, or rejected by others.<br><br>Conduct several 5-minute observations of a child who needs help learning to make friends. Review notes and summarize thoughts about the child.<br><br>Use what they learned to plans ways to help the child play with others over a 2-week period. Report what happened.<br><br>Share responses and chart feedback. If necessary, discuss possible causes of child's behavior with parents. | If possible, conduct classroom observations in order to learn about individual children and to assist teachers in identifying strategies to help children make friends.<br><br>Review teachers' observation notes, plans, and reports. Offer feedback.<br><br>Encourage teachers to try a variety of strategies with children who have difficulty playing with others. Consult with teachers periodically concerning children's interactions with each other. |

## Completing Module 9: Social (continued)

| Module Sections | What Teachers Do | What Trainers Do |
|---|---|---|
| **Reflecting on Your Learning** | Review the *Pre-Training Assessment*, add examples to the social development chart, summarize progress by answering questions, and consider curriculum connections and partnerships with families.<br><br>Share responses and chart feedback.<br><br>Complete the knowledge and competency assessments. | Discuss teacher's additions to their social development charts and their progress summaries.<br><br>Give and score the *Knowledge Assessment*.<br><br>Schedule an observation to complete the *Competency Assessment* for the module.<br><br>Provide feedback as teachers work on the assessments. |

### Strategies to Extend Learning

**Suggest that teachers ask a children's librarian to recommend children's books about caring behavior.** Teachers can place the books in the library area, read and discuss them with small groups or individual children, and offer activities and materials that allow children fully to explore explore the characters' feelings and actions.

**With a teacher, conduct several co-observations of children playing and engaged in activities, both indoors and outdoors.** Meet with the teacher to discuss what you saw and heard. Identify how children's social skills are related to development in other domains.

**Arrange for teachers to use a digital camera and printer.** Have teachers photograph the children during dramatic play, ideally play that extends over several days. Encourage teachers to use the photos to illustrate a book about what the children were doing. They can share the book with the children, to help them discuss the fun they had with their friends.

**Have teachers work with families to create traveling prop boxes focused on themes of interest to the children.** Each prop box can include general suggestions for encouraging children's play and specific ideas for children and parents to use the prop box together.

# Completing Module 10: Guidance

| Module Sections | What Teachers Do | What Trainers Do |
|---|---|---|
| **Overview**<br><br>**Your Own Self-Discipline**<br><br>**Pre-Training Assessment** | Read about self-discipline and using positive guidance to help children learn acceptable behavior.<br><br>Read and respond to questions about the three examples of how teachers guide children's behavior and about how self-discipline guides their behavior at work and home.<br><br>Complete the *Pre-Training Assessment* and list 3–5 skills to improve or topics to learn more about.<br><br>Share responses and chart feedback. | Observe teachers and review ongoing notes.<br><br>Discuss with teachers:<br><br>• responses to questions about the examples<br><br>• self-discipline experiences and how those experiences relate to helping children develop self-discipline<br><br>• the *Pre-Training Assessment*<br><br>When possible, evaluate *Pre-Training Assessment* responses by observing. |
| **Learning Activity A, Using Your Knowledge of Child Development to Guide Children's Behavior** | Read about typical preschool behavior and supportive teacher responses that minimize problems and help children develop self-discipline.<br><br>Complete the chart describing challenging behavior in the classroom, possible causes, and program changes that address the behavior.<br><br>Share responses and chart feedback. | Discuss how teachers organize their programs to minimize challenging behavior.<br><br>Review examples teachers recorded on their charts.<br><br>Share observations of how teachers help children develop self-discipline and how they respond to challenging behavior in the classroom. |
| **Learning Activity B, Guiding Children Toward Self-Disciplined Behavior** | Read about the differences between discipline and punishment, the connection between children's feelings and behavior, and positive guidance strategies.<br><br>Choose a child whose behavior Is challenging, consider possible reasons for the behavior, and describe their positive guidance strategies. Write about how they use what they learned to promote children's self-discipline.<br><br>Share responses and chart feedback. | Discuss the differences between discipline and punishment. Make sure teachers understand why it is important to help children develop self-discipline, a skill used throughout life.<br><br>If possible, observe teachers' use of positive guidance strategies and use notes to provide objective feedback.<br><br>Review teachers' observation summaries and highlight effective positive guidance strategies.<br><br>Encourage teachers to continue observing children to determine their needs and the reasons for their behavior, and to select guidance strategies appropriate for individual children and situations. |

## Completing Module 10: Guidance (continued)

| Module Sections | What Teachers Do | What Trainers Do |
|---|---|---|
| **Learning Activity C, Setting Rules and Limits** | Read about why children need a few simple rules, how to involve children in creating rules, when to individualize rules, using positive statements, and revising rules as children develop.<br><br>List their classroom rules, using positive phrases. Select one rule and answer questions about why it exists and how it is applied.<br><br>Share responses and chart feedback. | Discuss the lessons children learn from helping to make rules.<br><br>Ask teachers to describe instances when they individualized rules to meet children's needs.<br><br>Discuss the rules and teachers' explanations. Help teachers restate rules in positive terms, if needed.<br><br>Encourage teachers to set a schedule for reviewing rules to be sure they are still appropriate for the children in the group. |
| **Learning Activity D, Teaching Children to Use Problem-Solving Skills** | Read about the importance of encouraging children to solve social problems, strategies teachers use to teach problem-solving skills, and steps for solving problems with children.<br><br>Lead a group of children in solving a problem and describe what happened.<br><br>Share responses and chart feedback. | Discuss why problem-solving skills are important to the development of self-discipline.<br><br>Help teachers assist children in constructing appropriate approaches to social problems.<br><br>Provide feedback on the teachers' experiences with teaching problem-solving skills. |
| **Learning Activity E, Responding to Challenging Behavior** | Read about common challenging behavior of preschool children, probable causes, and the importance of working together with families.<br><br>Focus on a child whose behavior is challenging. Describe the behavior and how teachers usually respond.<br><br>Work with the child's family to develop a joint plan for responding to the behavior at home and at the program.<br><br>Implement the plan and evaluate the results.<br><br>Share responses and chart feedback. | If possible, observe children with challenging behavior and share notes and perceptions with their teachers.<br><br>If asked, help teachers prepare for the discussions with the children's families.<br><br>Help teachers implement classroom strategies for responding to the behavior. Consult regularly to discuss the children's progress.<br><br>Emphasize continued use of positive guidance to respond to challenging behavior. |

## Completing Module 10: Guidance (continued)

| Module Sections | What Teachers Do | What Trainers Do |
|---|---|---|
| **Reflecting on Your Learning** | Review responses to the *Pre-Training Assessment*, summarize progress by responding to questions, and consider curriculum connections and partnerships with families.<br><br>Share responses and chart feedback.<br><br>Complete the knowledge and competency assessments. | Discuss teachers' progress summaries.<br><br>Give and score the *Knowledge Assessment*.<br><br>Schedule an observation to complete the *Competency Assessment* for the module.<br><br>Provide feedback as teachers work on the assessments. |

### Strategies to Extend Learning

**Encourage teachers to meet regularly to discuss challenging behavior.** Identify possible causes of the behavior and plan strategies to help children learn acceptable ways to behave. Remind teachers to maintain the confidentiality of information about children and families.

**Use the information in this module and others to make a large chart summarizing the development of preschool children.** Post the chart where all teachers can see it. Next to the chart, post a piece of paper with the question, *How can you use this information to encourage self-discipline?* Ask teachers to write their suggestions and comment on each other's. Discuss the suggestions at a staff meeting.

**Sponsor a workshop for parents and teachers to discuss typical behaviors of preschool children.** Talk about what might cause challenging behavior and share appropriate guidance strategies to use at home and at the program. Help teachers plan the agenda and select key ideas to share with parents.

**Offer to audio- or videotape teachers' conversations and interactions with children.** Review the tape together and note the language and strategies teachers used to guide children's behavior.

**Work with teachers and families to observe children whose behavior interferes with full participation.** Help them plan ways to help the children learn acceptable behavior at home and at the program. If this approach is not effective, help the teachers and families work with early childhood mental health service providers.

## Completing Module 11: Families

| Module Sections | What Teachers Do | What Trainers Do |
|---|---|---|
| **Overview**<br><br>**Your Own Views About Families**<br><br>**Pre-Training Assessment** | Read about the importance of building positive partnerships with families, how teachers and families contribute to positive relationships, and how partnerships are built.<br><br>Read and answer questions about the three examples of how teachers work with families and about their own childhood experiences.<br><br>Complete the *Pre-Training Assessment* and list 3–5 skills to improve or topics to learn more about.<br><br>Share responses and chart feedback. | Observe teachers and review ongoing notes.<br><br>Discuss with teachers:<br><br>• responses to questions about the examples<br><br>• teachers' family experiences and how their views and pressures on families affect their work<br><br>• the *Pre-Training Assessment*<br><br>When possible, evaluate *Pre-Training Assessment* responses by observing. |
| **Learning Activity A, Building Partnerships With Families** | Read about types of information that families and teachers can share, ways to learn about families and exchange information, and helping children and families handle separations and reunions.<br><br>Identify the ways they help families and children handle separations and reunions.<br><br>Select a family they want to know better, decide the best approach, and describe what they learned and how they will use their understanding to build a partnership.<br><br>Share responses and chart feedback. | Observe interactions between teachers and family members. Give objective descriptions of their verbal and nonverbal communication.<br><br>Discuss what teachers learned about the families and how they were able to strengthen partnerships.<br><br>Suggest ways to strengthen partnerships with other families. |
| **Learning Activity B, Communicating With Families** | Read about introducing families to the program, using a variety of ways to communicate, and positive ways to address differences.<br><br>List the ways they keep families informed, identify and try a new way to communicate, and evaluate the new strategy.<br><br>Describe a time they had a difference of opinion or misunderstanding with a family and how they handled it.<br><br>Share responses and chart feedback. | Read and give feedback on teachers' communication strategies, such as newsletters, memos, handbooks, and bulletin boards.<br><br>Review the effectiveness of the teachers' strategies and suggest improvements, if necessary.<br><br>Suggest other ways to handle differences of opinion and misunderstandings. |

# Completing Module 11: Families (continued)

| Module Sections | What Teachers Do | What Trainers Do |
|---|---|---|
| **Learning Activity C, Providing Ways for Families to Participate** | Read about a variety of ways to involve families and how to make classroom participation meaningful.<br><br>List their approaches to family involvement.<br><br>Identify two families who have not been involved, try new approaches for involving them in the program, and report results.<br><br>Share responses and chart feedback. | Encourage teachers to ask families how they would like to be involved. Discuss the families' responses.<br><br>Review family involvement strategies and provide encouragement and suggestions. Offer to help get supplies, if necessary.<br><br>Help teachers set realistic expectations for family involvement. |
| **Learning Activity D, Planning and Participating in Conferences With Families** | Read about the goals of holding conferences with families, and how to plan and conduct them.<br><br>Schedule a conference with a family.<br><br>Prepare for the conference by organizing the child's portfolio, summarizing the child's developmental progress, and thinking about future objectives.<br><br>Conduct and evaluate the conference.<br><br>Share responses and chart feedback. | Discuss the importance of holding regular conferences to review each child's development thoroughly.<br><br>Help teachers prepare for conferences by reviewing planning forms and playing roles.<br><br>If possible, attend conferences. Offer feedback on tone, body language, shared information, and the overall effectiveness of the conference. Discuss teachers' feelings about the conferences. |
| **Learning Activity E, Providing Support to Families** | Read about recognizing when families are under stress, helping families locate resources, and sharing information on typical child growth and development with families.<br><br>Write about a situation when they offered support to a family.<br><br>Identify family support resources in their community and update or make a list of those resources.<br><br>Share responses and chart feedback. | Review the example about reaching out to families, offer feedback about teachers' experiences, and answer questions about supporting families.<br><br>Emphasize the importance of following program policies with regard to confidentiality and referrals.<br><br>Discuss signs of children's stress.<br><br>Discuss guidelines for talking about situations with a supervisor and referring a family to a professional. |

## Completing Module 11: Families (continued)

| Module Sections | What Teachers Do | What Trainers Do |
|---|---|---|
| **Reflecting on Your Learning** | Review responses to the *Pre-Training Assessment*, summarize progress by answering questions, and consider curriculum connections and partnerships with families.<br><br>Share responses and chart feedback.<br><br>Complete the knowledge and competency assessments. | Discuss teachers' progress summaries.<br><br>Give and score the *Knowledge Assessment*.<br><br>Schedule an observation to complete the competency assessment for the module.<br><br>Provide feedback as teachers work on the assessments. |

### Strategies to Extend Learning

**Lead a discussion on the similarities and differences between the families teachers grew up in and today's families.** Provide current statistics about families: single parent families, families with two working spouses, those with children from previous marriages, and families who live far away from their own parents and siblings.

**Provide information about signs of significant family stress.** Invite appropriate agencies to give presentations on responding when a family member appears to need immediate support. Develop a list of public and private, community and state organizations that provide services to families (e.g., hotlines and support groups).

**Work with community leaders to offer a workshop for teachers on diversity.** Discuss the different cultures of the program's families and ways to provide a program that values and responds to diversity.

**Conduct an informal family survey about receiving information from the program.** Ask all families to identify the types of information they would like to receive from the program and in what form (newsletters, informal chats, message centers, phone calls, bulletin boards, etc.).

# Completing Module 12: Program Management

| Module Sections | What Teachers Do | What Trainers Do |
|---|---|---|
| **Overview**<br><br>**Managing Your Own Life**<br><br>**Pre-Training Assessment** | Read about the management skills teachers use to plan, conduct, and evaluate their programs and why individualizing the program is an important management responsibility.<br><br>Read and respond to questions about the three examples of how teachers effectively manage the program and about how they manage their own lives.<br><br>Complete the *Pre-Training Assessment* and list 3–5 skills to improve or topics to learn more about.<br><br>Share responses and chart feedback. | Observe teachers and review ongoing notes.<br><br>Discuss with teachers:<br><br>• responses to questions about the examples<br><br>• their management experiences and challenges<br><br>• the *Pre-Training Assessment*<br><br>When possible, evaluate *Pre-Training Assessment* responses by observing. |
| **Learning Activity A, Collecting Information About Each Child** | Read about the importance of conducting and documenting ongoing, systematic, and complete observations. Review examples of observation notes that are objective and accurate and those that are not.<br><br>Observe a child for 5- to 10-minutes each day for a week and take notes. At least twice during the week, conduct a joint observation and compare notes. Analyze the notes to be sure they are objective, accurate, and complete.<br><br>Share responses and chart feedback. | Make sure teachers understand that observation is a critical skill for early childhood professionals. Teachers will observe children while completing the modules and throughout their early childhood careers.<br><br>If possible, conduct and discuss at least two co-observations of the child. Especially when this is not possible, make sure teachers conduct joint observations with colleagues or supervisors.<br><br>Discuss examples of accurate and objective notes that do not use labels.<br><br>Provide support and assistance if teachers need to repeat the activity. |
| **Learning Activity B, Organizing and Using Portfolios** | Read about creating portfolios of children's work, the kinds of work samples to include, how to store the samples, and how to use them with children and families.<br><br>During a 2-week period, collect items to include in a portfolio for one of the children observed in *Learning Activity A*. Develop a system for organizing and storing the portfolio. Describe the portfolio, including how each item documents the child's development.<br><br>Share responses and chart feedback. | Explain the reasons why portfolios are an effective way to track progress and plan individualized programs.<br><br>Review the portfolio descriptions and suggest additional work samples.<br><br>Suggest ways to involve families and children in selecting items to include in portfolios.<br><br>Discuss the contents, organization, and use of the portfolios that the teachers compile. |

## Completing Module 12: Program Management (continued)

| Module Sections | What Teachers Do | What Trainers Do |
|---|---|---|
| **Learning Activity C, Meeting Individual Needs and Interests** | Read about what it means to individualize the program, strategies for individualizing different elements of the program, and meeting the needs of children with disabilities.<br><br>Select the same child from *Learning Activity A* and *B* and summarize what they learned. Plan ways to meet the child's individual needs and build on the child's strengths, skills, and interests.<br><br>Share responses and chart feedback. | Help teachers analyze their observations and portfolios and what they learned about the children's strengths, interests, and needs.<br><br>Review and discuss ways to meet each child's individual needs and build on each child's interests.<br><br>Encourage teachers to establish a system for conducting and recording regular observations of all the children. |
| **Learning Activity D, Working as a Team to Plan and Evaluate the Program** | Read about long-range and weekly planning, evaluating the program, and changing plans to reflect evaluation results.<br><br>As a team, review information about the children in their group. Develop, implement, and evaluate a weekly plan.<br><br>Share responses and chart feedback. | Review and provide feedback on weekly plans.<br><br>If appropriate, attend planning and evaluation meetings with teachers and their colleagues.<br><br>Help teachers assess the effectiveness of the format and approach they now use for weekly planning. If changes are needed, offer to assist. |
| **Reflecting on Your Learning** | Review responses to the *Pre-Training Assessment*, respond to questions summarizing progress, and consider curriculum connections and partnerships with families.<br><br>Share responses and chart feedback.<br><br>Complete the knowledge and competency assessments. | Discuss teachers' progress summaries.<br><br>Give and score the *Knowledge Assessment*.<br><br>Schedule an observation to complete the *Competency Assessment* for the module.<br><br>Provide feedback as teachers work on the assessments. |

### Strategies to Extend Learning

**Introduce a variety of observation and documentation formats.** Include formats such as anecdotal recordkeeping, time sampling, event sampling, rating scales, and skills checklists. Encourage teachers to pick the instrument or format that best serves a particular need, such as observing to assess children's developmental levels, evaluating the environment, documenting children's progress in a specific area, or keeping records to discuss with families.

**Provide a video camera and tripod that teachers may use indoors or outdoors.** Encourage them to let the camera run, cinema verité style. Together, view what the camera recorded. Discuss what the children did, materials and skills they used, how they interacted with each other and with the teachers, and how the teachers responded. Help teachers identify their instructional styles; different methods used for different purposes and with different children; and the ways children respond to teachers' statements, questions, and actions.

**Organize a group of teachers to evaluate whether their program's management policies and practices meet children's needs.** Ask them to suggest changes or additions to planning documents, portfolio collection procedures, and assessment and reporting systems to make sure they are useful. Have group members prepare a written report about suggested program management changes and meet with the director to present their findings.

**Plan a series of workshops on the managerial skills that teachers use.** Discuss skills such as team building, observing and taking notes, analyzing information, managing time, using a planning cycle, and recordkeeping.

# Completing Module 13: Professionalism

| Module Sections | What Teachers Do | What Trainers Do |
|---|---|---|
| **Overview**<br><br>**Viewing Yourself as a Professional**<br><br>**Pre-Training Assessment** | Read about the standards, ethics, and obligations of the early childhood profession.<br><br>Read and respond to questions about the three examples of how teachers maintain a commitment to professionalism; reflect on what it means to be a professional; and think about the interests, knowledge, skills, and style they bring to their work.<br><br>Complete the *Pre-Training Assessment* and list 3–5 skills to improve or topics to learn more about.<br><br>Share responses and chart feedback. | Observe teachers and review ongoing notes.<br><br>Discuss with teachers:<br><br>• responses to questions about the examples<br><br>• their understandings of themselves as professionals, including the skills and talents they bring to their work<br><br>• the *Pre-Training Assessment*<br><br>When possible, evaluate *Pre-Training Assessment* responses by observing. |
| **Learning Activity A, Striving to Meet the Standards of the Profession** | Read about the standards that guide the early childhood profession.<br><br>Select two NAEYC position papers and identify ideas/strategies that are of interest to them. Describe how those ideas are being implemented in their program.<br><br>Share responses and chart feedback. | If necessary, help teachers obtain copies of the position papers.<br><br>Discuss the ideas teachers chose and how they are implementing them in their programs. |
| **Learning Activity B, Continuing to Gain New Knowledge and Skills** | Read about the four stages of professional development for teachers, the benefits of continued learning, joining professional groups, and other ways to continue professional growth.<br><br>Select and learn about one early childhood professional organization.<br><br>Develop a professional development plan to expand their knowledge about a topic that interests them and identify resources that will help them learn.<br><br>Share responses and chart feedback. | Encourage teachers to build time for training and skill development into their schedules.<br><br>Provide information on relevant classes, lectures, and conferences.<br><br>Review teachers' professional development plans and offer support, if needed. |

## Completing Module 13: Professionalism (continued)

| Module Sections | What Teachers Do | What Trainers Do |
|---|---|---|
| **Learning Activity C, Demonstrating Ethical Behavior In Your Work** | Read about the NAEYC *Code of Ethical Conduct*, examples of professional and unprofessional behavior, and situations that present ethical dilemmas.<br><br>List ways their behavior exemplifies the ethical principles of teaching.<br><br>Share responses and chart feedback. | Discuss examples of professional behavior.<br><br>Review observation notes to identify and share examples of teachers' commitment to ethical principles. Discuss ethical issues as they arise.<br><br>Encourage teachers by acknowledging their conscientious work habits, ethical behavior, and continuing professional growth. |
| **Learning Activity D, Talking About the Value of Your Work** | Read about the importance of sharing their knowledge of early childhood care and education with others and about ways to advocate for change.<br><br>Answer questions explaining the value of their work and their ideas about improving the early childhood field.<br><br>Identify and take two advocacy steps and report the results of their efforts.<br><br>Share responses and chart feedback. | Explain the importance of advocating in a way that is comfortable for them. Suggest ways they can talk about the value of their work in the larger community.<br><br>Review advocacy plans and offer to assist in implementing them. |
| **Reflecting on Your Learning** | Review responses to the *Pre-Training Assessment*, summarize progress by answering questions, and consider curriculum connections and partnerships with families.<br><br>Share responses and chart feedback.<br><br>Complete the knowledge and competency assessments. | Discuss teachers' progress summaries.<br><br>Give and score the *Knowledge Assessment*.<br><br>Schedule an observation to complete the *Competency Assessment* for the module.<br><br>Provide feedback as teachers work on the assessments. |

### Strategies to Extend Learning

**Facilitate a discussion about issues affecting the health and well-being of children and families in the community or state.** Discuss ways in which teachers can become advocates.

**Build a comprehensive lending library of professional materials.** Include books, journals, and audiovisual materials on early childhood development and education, cultural competence, including children with disabilities, involving families, and other topics of interest to teachers.

**Encourage teachers to be partners in each other's professional development.** They might share rides and child care, plan and lead workshops together, share resources, and otherwise help each other achieve their professional goals.

**Conduct workshops on ethical issues.** Consider topics such as discipline methods or how to respond when teachers and parents disagree about appropriate practices. Ask teachers to suggest topics they would like to discuss.

**Discuss with teachers the next steps in their professional development.** For example, will they seek a credential, attend college courses, enroll in a degree program, or continue independent-study? Help teachers understand how the *Caring for Preschool* modules fit their plans for ongoing professional growth.

# Chapter 3

# Using the Modules in Courses and Workshops

When you use the *Caring for Preschool Children* modules in group settings such as courses and workshops, consider the personal nature of the training program. In their *Skill-Building Journals*, teachers report their personal impressions and experiences, as well as how they apply information in their own settings. You will learn a great deal about each person and have a unique opportunity to adapt your training to address their individual interests and needs. Also keep in mind the value of observing teachers while they work with children. While group sessions can provide valuable information about each teacher's progress, the training is most effective when it includes individualized, on-site feedback and support based on systematic, objective observations. If you teach a college course, you may already observe teachers as part of a practicum. Use such visits to observe and to provide support and feedback, and use one to administer each *Competency Assessment*. The chart on page 11 shows how the 13 modules in *Caring for Preschool Children* might be used for a series of college courses.

This chapter provides logistical tips to help you plan group sessions. It also offers suggestions to make people feel comfortable about participating. A variety of training approaches are described so you can use those that fit your style and what you know about the teachers who will be attending your sessions. We offer suggestions about evaluating the training and include a sample evaluation form in the Appendix. We also provide a sample training plan for module 10, *Guidance*, to show how you might design a series of sessions on any of the 13 modules.

## Attending to Logistics

Group sessions are most successful when they are well planned and everything is in place before participants arrive for training. What may seem like simple details can either enhance or get in the way of learning. Here are some pointers for making logistical arrangements that support comfortable and productive training sessions.

- Schedule sessions at times that are convenient for teachers. For example, you might conduct them after the children leave for the day, at naptime, or, if possible, on in-service days. Teachers have steady demands on their professional and personal time. Accommodating their schedules is respectful, and it makes high attendance easier.

- Notify participants of the date, time, and location of the training. If appropriate, include directions to the building and room where the session will be held. Provide an agenda and other preparatory materials in advance.

- Offer refreshments. Healthy snacks and hot or cold drinks refresh minds and energize participants. A table cloth, even fresh flowers, can make the room inviting.

- Arrange for tables that seat 4–5 people and adult-size chairs that provide comfortable support.

- Prepare or arrange for needed materials and equipment in advance. This includes audiovisual equipment, videos, chart paper, markers, tape, chalk, handouts, and evaluation forms. Check to make sure the equipment works and that there are replacement bulbs, extension cords, and adapters on hand.

- Arrange the furniture before the participants arrive in a pattern that suits your training style. Many trainers prefer circles, semi-circles, or small tables because these arrangements encourage participant discussions.

- Display name tags, sign-in sheets, agendas, and reference materials in areas readily accessible to participants.

- Check to be sure the room temperature is comfortable before starting the session. An overheated room can put an audience to sleep more quickly than a boring speaker, but participants will have a hard time focusing if the room is too cold.

By attending to these few logistical concerns, you'll be able to focus on the content of the training rather than searching for extension cords or a building engineer to adjust the temperature. Preparation goes a long way when it comes to training.

# Facilitating Group Sessions

One of your most important roles is to help all participants feel comfortable enough to express their ideas, share experiences, and ask questions. Some teachers find participation in group discussions and activities intimidating, and even experienced teachers may be reluctant to speak in a group. Here are some tips for facilitating training sessions that will help participants feel comfortable about participating.

## At the Start of the Session

- Greet participants by name as they enter. Welcome them to the session.

- Discuss the rules and guidelines, describe the plan for breaks, and say when the session will end.

- Point out the location of restrooms, telephones, and water fountains. This will minimize interruptions once the session starts.

- Provide an overview of the session. Explain the goals and objectives, describe the content and activities, and refer to the handouts. Invite participants to share their own expectations. Training is more effective when the group understands and shares a commitment to the goals and objectives.

- Remind participants that they are responsible for their own learning. Explain that everyone will take something different from the session, depending on what ideas are most important to them, how much they contribute, and whether they integrate and use what they learn.

- Underscore the importance of the topics and skills to be covered. Emphasize that the purpose of training is to help teachers do their jobs better and enhance their professional development.

## During Discussions

- Encourage participants to listen actively and to express their opinions. Acknowledge that sharing ideas and experiences in a group may feel a little uncomfortable at first. Note that all ideas are valuable and there is usually more than one right way to approach a topic. Avoid embarrassing participants by forcing each person to contribute.

- Look for body-language cues. They may alert you to discomfort with the subject matter (squirming), shyness about contributing (avoiding eye contact), or anger (turning the entire body away). Try to respond to what you see.

- Guide participants to reach compromises or at least to respect different points of view. This is particularly important when conflicts or disagreements occur.

- Encourage participants to ask questions. Answering their questions helps you explain information and eliminate misunderstandings. It is often helpful to rephrase questions to clarify what is being asked. Redirect some questions to the group to help participants find answers on the basis of their own experiences and expertise. If you can't answer a question, say so and explain that you will try to find the answer before the next session. Be sure to follow up.

- Ask questions to engage teachers in dialogue. At times, it is appropriate to use both closed questions ("What happened when you handled the situation that way last time?") and open-ended questions ("What are some other ways you could handle the situation?"). Refer a question to the entire group if you sense that an in-depth discussion would be beneficial. ("That's a tough problem. Does anyone have a suggestion?")

## Throughout the Session

- Draw on participants' experiences. Training is more meaningful when participants relate concepts to personal situations and experiences.

- Emphasize skill development rather than rote learning of correct responses. Learning is the process of assimilating new information and using it to improve skills.

- Encourage participants to make interpretations and draw conclusions. Effective training provides background information; data; and examples participants use to identify patterns or trends, make generalizations, and draw conclusions.

- Adjust the agenda to meet the needs of participants. Use a mixture of planned and spontaneous activities and content, just as you take advantage of teachable moments with children.

- Use small-group activities to discuss feelings. Consider using role-playing, simulations, or problem-solving assignments.

- Give clear instructions for activities. Repeat them if necessary. Move around the room to assist individuals or groups who are confused about the tasks.

- Review and summarize each section of the training before moving on to the next. At the end of the session, lead a summary discussion and answer participants' questions.

- Be available during breaks to discuss issues and topics. Some participants may prefer to share their views with you one-on-one rather than in front of the whole group.

# Varying Training Approaches

There are many training techniques to consider as you plan group training based on the *Caring for Preschool Children* modules. Select training techniques that reflect current knowledge about how adults learn, address the needs of the teachers who will participate, and are consistent with your own preferences and training philosophy. For example, you may want to plan mini-lectures as part of your workshops if you are comfortable giving presentations. On the other hand, you may rely on group discussions if are unsure of your skills as a lecturer. Your range of training approaches should meet participants' varied learning styles.

Include a variety of activities and use different kinds of media when possible. A balance of training techniques maintains the group's interest and promotes greater retention and application of skills and content. To encourage participants' active involvement, consider using role-playing, small group analysis, discussion, and case studies. These techniques allow participants to apply training concepts, principles, and strategies to real-life situations.

Try those of the following training ideas that suit your style and what you know about the participants. Make modifications as necessary.

## Written Materials

When using the modules for training, make sure that every participant has a copy of the *Skill-Building Journal*. Participants will also need to have access to *Caring for Preschool* so they can do the readings. You can supplement these resources with articles from professional journals, a list of Web sites, or some of the resources recommended at the back of the book.

## Audiovisuals

Audiovisuals can be very effective training tools. Videotapes that show realistic and relevant scenes from early childhood programs are especially effective. Your own slides or videotapes of programs can be used to illustrate ideas covered in training.

Some trainers use visual displays, such as PowerPoint presentations or overhead transparencies, to reinforce the key points of a lecture and introduce discussion topics and questions. Either format can include both words and pictures, but PowerPoint presentations offer more creative and sophisticated options. Here are some suggestions for developing slides and transparencies.

- Include key words and phrases only.

- Use large type so participants can read the screen from anywhere in the room.

- Be sure there is sufficient contrast between the background color and lettering so text is easy to read.

- Keep illustrations or graphs simple.

- Use color to highlight key information.

- Use visuals, such as photographs, to introduce and reinforce content.

## Problem-Solving Activities

One popular and effective training technique is group problem solving. Brainstorming solutions to realistic problems can energize a group and generate many ideas. Brainstorming is designed to separate the creation of ideas from their evaluation. This strategy works best in groups of 5–12 persons and requires someone to serve as the recorder and someone to be the facilitator who leads the group through the process. The rules for brainstorming are as follows:

- All ideas are listed; no critical remarks are allowed.

- *Hitchhiking* is allowed; if one participant can improve upon or combine previously mentioned ideas, so much the better.

- *Freewheeling* is encouraged; even outlandish ideas keep the group momentum going.

- There is no limit to the number of ideas that may be included. The more ideas that participants generate, the more likely viable solutions will evolve.

- Discussion and evaluation are postponed until participants have finished generating ideas.

Brainstorming could be used to answer questions such as the following:

- Why do children misbehave?

- What factors work against families' participation in the program?

- What are the best ways to keep children engaged in listening to a story?

## Case Studies

Case studies are realistic examples of situations related to a particular topic. The chief advantage of this method is that it helps participants apply what they learn through lectures or assigned readings to the real world. Many of the vignettes and examples in the modules can be used to develop case studies.

Distribute a copy of the case study to each participant or small group and allow time for it to be read. Participants can discuss the study in pairs, small groups, or the full group. Depending on the case study, ask leading questions to stimulate thinking. Here are some examples:

- What went wrong?

- What worked well?

- How could this problem be avoided in the future?

- How could this individual build on his or her success?

- What did the children learn from this experience?

- What feedback would you provide to this individual?

## Role-Playing

Role-playing presents opportunities to act out real-life situations in a risk-free environment. By seeing things from another perspective, participants gain insight into various ways to approach a problem or issue. Keep in mind that some adults are very uncomfortable playing different roles and may prefer to watch. A more comfortable way to conduct role-playing is to form groups of three, with two persons assuming roles and the third person observing and giving feedback.

## Discussion Techniques

Trainers can use fishbowl, fantasy, and visualization techniques to stimulate discussions. For the **fishbowl**, divide participants into two groups, forming inner and outer rings of a circle. Give participants in the inner group an assignment based on the content of the training. For example, the inner group might discuss the difference between discipline and punishment. While the inner group discusses this problem for five to ten minutes, the outer group observes. At the end of the allotted time, the two groups switch roles. At the conclusion of the second discussion, both groups comment on what they observed. This technique can stimulate discussion among participants who are reluctant to speak in a large group.

Fantasy and visualization are techniques used to draw on right brain (creative thinking) powers. **Fantasy** techniques usually ask participants to reflect on "What if . . .?" situations, for example, "What if you had unlimited financial resources? How would you equip your room?" Participants can list the materials and equipment in an ideal inventory and then compare the ideal to reality to see where compromises are appropriate. Conversely, you can fantasize about worst-case scenarios: "What if your budget were cut by 50 percent?"

**Visualization** allows participants to use their imaginations to think about a task and relate it to past or future experiences. For example, you might ask participants to think about a time when they had to do something that made them uncomfortable. What were the circumstances? How did they feel? What did they do to relieve their discomfort? What will they do if it ever happens again? You might use visualization if you sense that participants are uncomfortable dealing with particular situations, such as explaining to parents that children may not attend the program when they have a contagious illness.

## Mini-Lectures

Mini-lectures are useful when you are covering important points that you want everyone to understand. Provide a handout summarizing the key ideas or refer participants to where the ideas are discussed in *Caring for Preschool Children*. Illustrate key concepts with visuals such as PowerPoint presentations, overhead transparencies, or notes recorded on chart paper.

At the close of the mini-lecture, review the key points. You can restate them yourself, invite the group to summarize, conduct a review discussion, or lead an activity related to the material. These steps allow participants to assimilate the ideas and construct their own understandings. They can relate it to their own thinking, decide what it means to them, and consider how it affects their work with children and families.

## Group Discussions

**Small groups** of 4–6 participants are ideal for discussion and sharing. For participants who are reluctant to speak in a large group, small-group activities are more comfortable. Small-group interactions offer more intimate connections among group members, encourage the active involvement of all participants, and help them build networks and relationships.

To form small groups, try one of the following methods:

- Ask participants to form groups of a specified size.

- Have participants count off (e.g., up to 5) and then group persons with the same number.

- Distribute cards with pictures, stickers, or numbers and have participants match cards and group accordingly.

- Assign participants to groups according to roles or ability.

- Distribute individual pieces of 4- to 6-piece puzzles. Participants form groups by assembling the puzzles.

- Place pictures or names of classifiable objects in a bag (for example, furniture, clothing, animals). Have participants choose a card and then form a group with others whose objects fit the same category.

Here are some strategies for using small groups effectively:

- Give clear instructions for the task and check to be sure participants understand what they are to do.

- Seat participants together and away from other groups.

- Give 3- and 1-minute warnings before ending discussions.

- Ask groups to report to the whole group in round-robin style. Each group takes a turn reporting one or two ideas until all new ideas are listed. This prevents repetition, and the first group does not report all the popular answers.

- Reporting to the full group may not always be necessary, especially if you think that each group's discussion was thorough. Ask if there were any highlights or important insights any group would like to share.

**Large-group** discussions can be used to break up a mini-lecture, discuss reactions to a videotape, and give participants an opportunity to contribute to and learn from their peers. If an entire group is 15 persons or less, discussions involving the whole group allow members to hear all the ideas.

The trainer's role is to facilitate communication and make sure everyone can hear. It is important to receive participants' comments without judgment. If a statement indicates a lack of understanding, use the next break to discuss it with the participant. If a statement is incorrect, provide the correct information as diplomatically as possible: "Many people think that is true; however, the state health office recommends . . ."

During large-group discussions, some participants might be frustrated because they feel ignored, misunderstood, or unable to participate. It is important to observe both the behavior of the group as a whole and that of individuals. When a participant's comments have apparently been misunderstood, paraphrase and clarify them for the whole group: "What I hear you saying is. . . Am I right?" This strategy allows participants to restate their comments and continue to participate.

# Evaluating Training

Trainers want to know if their training has been effective. Did the participants increase their understanding of the content? Do they feel capable of implementing what they have learned? Do they think the session was beneficial? Did they gain skills or change approaches?

To answer these questions, you can use group or individual training evaluations. The following are two examples of evaluation techniques that involve the whole group in offering feedback during a training session.

**Pluses and Wishes:** On chart paper or a blackboard, draw a chart with two columns. Label one "pluses" and the other "wishes." Ask, "What did you like about this training? What were the pluses? What do you wish the training had included but did not?" Responses are likely to vary from concerns about logistics ("The chairs were uncomfortable.") to comments about the content ("I can use the ideas for making prop boxes immediately.").

**Gets/Wants Chart:** On chart paper or a blackboard, make a chart with four quadrants, like the axes on a graph. Label the sections as in the following example.

| Got—Wanted | Didn't Get—Wanted |
|---|---|
| *Suggestions for encouraging creativity* <br><br> *Opportunities to learn from other teachers* | *Ideas for new materials* <br><br> *Refreshments* |
| **Got—Didn't Want** | **Didn't Get—Didn't Want** |
| *Video I'd seen before* <br><br> *Role-playing* | |

As you discuss each quadrant, ask participants to provide examples of parts of the training they "got and wanted," "got but didn't want," and "didn't get but wanted." When you get to the last quadrant, explain that it doesn't need to be addressed because the items must be irrelevant to their jobs ("You didn't get this information, but it doesn't matter because you didn't want it!"). See the chart above for examples of the types of responses participants might offer. When planning future training, you can review the responses and decide if you should continue to offer the things they "got and wanted," provide things they "didn't get and wanted," and eliminate the things they "got and didn't want!"

Individual questionnaires completed at the end of the training can help you assess which parts of the training were well received. (A sample training evaluation questionnaire is provided in the Appendix.) For example, did participants like group exercises but dislike the mini-lectures? Did they think too much content was presented in too short a time? Review participants' reactions to answer questions such as these:

- How effectively did the session accomplish its objectives?

- How relevant was the content to the participants' jobs?

- What changes to the format, content, activities, or techniques are needed?

- Do participants need more in-depth coverage of the topic?

Participant evaluations are a valuable tool for assessing whether training needs have been met. As you review the results, though, bear in mind that not everyone is always going to be satisfied with training. Some variations in answers are to be expected, and you should revise your approach only if warranted.

# Sample Training Plan for Module 10, *Guidance*

When planning a series of group sessions based on the modules in *Caring for Preschool Children*, think about the training techniques you will use, how you will facilitate discussions, and how you will evaluate the sessions. Before each session, ask participants to submit their completed *Skill-Building Journal* forms for your review and written comments. Explain that you will return their work, with your comments, at the beginning of the session. Be sure to allow time for participants to take a quick look at your comments before the session begins. Develop a plan to meet individually with teachers who would like assistance in completing an activity or who want to discuss your feedback.

An example of a plan for a series of group sessions on Module 10, *Guidance*, follows. This plan can be adapted to address individual interests and training needs. A Planning Form for Group Sessions is in the Appendix. You may find this form helpful as a framework for planning group sessions on any of the *Caring for Preschool Children* modules.

# Sample Training Plan for Module 10, Guidance

## Overview

**Open the Session**

Begin with an open-ended question such as the following:

- What do you consider when choosing a guidance strategy?

- How do children learn what behaviors are accepted and valued by others?

- What strategies do you and your colleagues use to minimize challenging behavior?

- What difficulties do you experience in guiding the behavior of individual children?

- What does your discipline policy tell families?

**Discuss the Key Topics**

Introduce the three major areas of competence that teachers develop to guide children's behavior:

- minimizing problem behavior and encouraging self-discipline

- using positive guidance to help each child learn acceptable behavior

- helping children express their strong feelings in acceptable ways

Lead a discussion about the key topics by using questions such as the following:

- How do children use self-discipline?

     **Possible responses:**

     *They identify and monitor their emotions.*

     *They make decisions for themselves.*

     *They solve their own problems.*

     *They correct their mistakes.*

     *They behave appropriately without anyone's telling them what to do.*

     *They take responsibility for their own actions.*

     *They learn to follow classroom rules.*

- What are some of the reasons children misbehave?

    **Possible responses:**

    *They don't know what they are supposed to do.*

    *They want to test the limits set by adults.*

    *They respond to a strong feeling without thinking about the consequences.*

    *The program (schedule, activities, routines, and so on) doesn't meet their needs.*

    *The rules at home are different from those at the program.*

    *A situation at home or at the program is upsetting them.*

    *They need attention but don't know how to ask for it in a positive way.*

    *They miss their parents.*

    *They are tired, hungry, or ill.*

    *They feel afraid or insecure.*

    *They want to do things for themselves.*

## Review the Three Examples

Review the example of how teachers minimize problem behavior and encourage self-discipline.

- Ask participants to offer examples of how different aspects of their program promote self-discipline.

- Discuss the example and responses to the questions in the *Skill-Building Journal.*

- Invite participants to describe a similar situation in their program, how they handled it, and what happened.

Review the example of how a teacher uses positive guidance to help a child learn acceptable behavior.

- Ask participants to give examples of positive guidance they have used to help individual children gain self-discipline.

- Discuss the example and responses to the questions in the *Skill-Building Journal.*

- Invite participants to describe a similar situation in their program, how they handled it, and what happened.

Review the example of how a teacher helps a child express her strong feelings in an acceptable way.

- Ask participants to describe their approach to helping children express their strong feelings in acceptable ways.

- Discuss the example and responses to the questions in the *Skill-Building Journal.*

- Invite participants to describe a similar situation in their program, how they handled it, and what happened.

### Discuss Your Own Self-Discipline

Lead a discussion about the ways adults use self-discipline, using questions such as the following to encourage participation:

- How does self-discipline affect your own behavior?

  **Possible responses:**

  *It helps me feel good about myself and my abilities.*

  *It helps me contribute to my family and community.*

  *It lets me respond automatically because I have learned and value certain rules of behavior.*

- How does your self-discipline affect your work with children?

  **Possible responses:**

  *Modeling self-discipline helps children learn acceptable ways to behave.*

  *Being able to control my emotions and my behavior leads to greater self-esteem, which may make me more effective and skilled.*

### End the Session

Answer questions. Schedule individual meetings or phone conferences to discuss responses, review the teachers' *Pre-Training Assessments* and their lists of skills to improve or topics to learn more about.

## Learning Activity A

## Using Your Knowledge of Child Development to Guide Children's Behavior

### Open the Session

Ask participants how child development knowledge helps them guide children's behavior.

> Possible responses:
>
> *I am realistic about what children can do, so I don't expect too much or too little.*
>
> *I can provide guidance that helps children learn appropriate behavior and gain self-discipline.*
>
> *I can adapt the program to meet the children's developmental levels rather than expecting the children to adapt to a program that doesn't meet their needs.*

### Discuss the Text

Review the content of the chart, Developmental Characteristics and Teacher Responses. For each item in the column titled, *Preschool children . . .*, ask participants to share examples of supportive responses they use in their programs.

### Review the Activity

Discuss the problem behaviors, possible causes, and suggested solutions listed by participants on their activity charts. Emphasize the important connections between preschoolers' developmental characteristics and the guidance strategies that minimize problem behaviors and help children learn self-discipline. As appropriate, offer examples from your own observations of how teachers guided the behavior of preschool children.

### Offer Additional Resources and Activities

Provide poster board and markers so participants can make charts similar to those in this learning activity. Suggest posting them in a central area, such as the staff lounge, so they and their colleagues can add additional examples of what preschool children are like and ways to use this information to minimize problem behaviors and promote self-discipline.

### End the Session

Offer to review and discuss the completed activity during individual meetings or phone conferences.

Introduce the next learning activity.

# Learning Activity B

## Guiding Children Toward Self-Disciplined Behavior

**Open the Session**

Begin by asking participants to think about the differences between punishment and discipline. Use the following prompts to facilitate a discussion:

- Punishment teaches children . . .

- Discipline teaches children . . .

- Over time, punishment often leads to . . .

- Over time, discipline often leads to . . .

Review the following key points:

- Punishment imposes a physical or emotional penalty. When punished or threatened with punishment, children may behave because they are afraid of what might happen to them if they don't. Punishment may stop the inappropriate behavior temporarily, but it doesn't teach children what to do. Instead, it may reinforce their bad feelings about themselves.

- Discipline means guiding and directing children toward acceptable behavior. It teaches children what is acceptable and helps them learn to solve problems and behave in positive ways in the future. The most important goal of discipline is to help children learn to control their own behavior.

- Children learn self-discipline through daily interactions with adults and each other. It takes a long time to guide children's behavior in ways that promote self-discipline, but it is time well spent. Children who are self-disciplined tend to be more successful in school and in life.

**Discuss the Text**

Ask questions such as the following to encourage participants to share their ideas:

- What might children be feeling and trying to communicate when they misbehave?

    **Possible responses:**

    *I feel lonely because . . . .*

    *I am angry because . . . .*

    *I am afraid the other children will laugh at me.*

    *I want to be good at something.*

    *I need some limits.*

    *I can't do what you asked me to do.*

- What can you do to help children understand and express their feelings?

    **Possible responses:**

    *Observe children and recognize the signs that a child is upset.*

    *Suggest a soothing activity that might help a child feel better.*

    *Provide time and space to help a child calm down.*

    *Help children find the words to express themselves.*

    *Pay attention to what a child needs rather than what the child is doing.*

Ask participants to remember when they were children. Have them focus on how they felt when an adult spoke quietly, using a firm tone of voice. Then ask the following question:

- What are some guidelines for using words to guide children's behavior?

    **Possible responses:**

    *Use a natural but firm tone of voice so children feel safe and cared for.*

    *Get close enough to children so you can speak at a normal volume.*

    *Crouch or kneel at a child's level when having a private discussion.*

    *Look into a child's eyes and gently touch an arm or shoulder.*

    *Give the child your full attention and make sure you have his or her attention.*

    *Be sensitive to cultural differences.*

## Review the Activity

Ask pairs or small groups to share what they learned while examining ways they guided the behavior of an individual child. Ask them to discuss how the positive guidance strategies they used met the criteria listed below.

- They were based on realistic expectations for the child's behavior.

- They reflect an understanding of child development.

- They reflect an understanding of the child's unique characteristics.

- They were individualized to match the situation and the child's skills and needs.

Ask each pair or group to present the main points of their discussion. Address questions and any areas of disagreement.

**Offer Additional Resources and Activities**

Share articles, books, Web sites, and other resources that stress the importance of using a developmental approach to guidance and that offer effective strategies. Discuss ways to involve families as partners in helping children learn self-discipline.

**End the Session**

Ask participants if they have access to tape recorders. Suggest that they tape themselves interacting with children.

Offer to review and discuss the completed activity during individual meetings or phone conferences.

Introduce the next learning activity.

## Learning Activity C

## Setting Rules and Limits

### Open the Session

Ask participants to share a rule from their programs. Write the rules on chart paper. The ask the following questions:

- How do these rules help children stay safe? …learn? …gain self-discipline?

- How do these rules support teachers so they can implement a developmentally appropriate program?

- How do you know when a rule is effective? How do you know when it needs to be changed?

- How are children involved in setting rules?

- How do you help children understand the reasons for the rules?

### Discuss the Text

Ask questions such as the following to encourage participants to share ideas:

- Why is it important to have rules and limits?

  **Possible responses:**

  *Rules and limits help teachers and children agree on what behavior is acceptable and what is not.*

  *Children feel safe when they know adults will enforce rules and limits consistently. When children feel safe, they are more likely to explore and experiment.*

- Why is it important to have just enough rules?

  **Possible responses:**

  *When there are too many rules, children can't remember them and they feel unsure of themselves.*

  *When there are too few rules, the environment might be disorderly and the children might be unsafe.*

  *Children feel a sense of mastery when they can remember and follow a few simple rules.*

- Why is it important to involve children in creating rules?

  **Possible responses:**

  *Children are more likely to remember and follow rules they have helped to create.*

  *Children are more likely to understand why rules are needed if they helped set them.*

  *When children understand the reasons for rules, they are more likely to follow them.*

- *Caring for Preschool Children* presents an example about changing a rule to meet an individual child's special need. When have you found it necessary to bend a classroom rule? What happened?

- Why is it important to review and revise the rules periodically?

  **Possible responses:**

  *As children grow and mature they can handle more freedom, activities, and responsibility.*

  *Rules that were once needed to keep children safe may now get in the way of their growth and independence.*

## Review the Activity

Have teachers share the rules they listed in this activity and check to see if they are written as positive statements that remind children of what to do.

Ask volunteers to share some of their classroom rules and their responses to the *Skill-Building Journal* questions about their rules. Stress the importance of respecting and acknowledging children's feelings.

## Additional Resources and Activities

Have participants work in pairs to share and discuss their program rules. Provide paper so participants can rewrite rules as needed to state them positively. Also encourage them to identify rules that might be unnecessary or that might need revision to reflect children's growth and maturity.

## End the Session

Offer to review and discuss the completed activity during individual meetings or phone conferences.

Introduce the next learning activity.

## Learning Activity D

## Teaching Children to Use Problem-Solving Skills

### Open the Session

Have participants think of a time when someone stepped in to solve a problem for them. Ask the following questions:

- How did it feel to have the problem taken away?

- What would you do if the problem came up again?

Next, ask participants to relate their experiences and feelings to how children might feel when adults step in to solve their problems.

### Discuss the Text

Ask questions such as the following to encourage dialogue among participants:

- Why is it important to take the time to teach children problem-solving skills?

    **Possible responses:**

    *Children can use problem-solving skills now and in the future.*

    *Children who see themselves as problem solvers are more likely to be successful in school and life.*

- How can you encourage children to learn and use problem-solving skills?

    **Possible responses:**

    *Be patient. Allow enough time for children to try and try again.*

    *Accept and respect children's responses, even when they are different from those adults might devise.*

    *Allow time for thinking. Children need time to collect their thoughts before expressing them.*

    *Offer help in small increments. Let children learn from their mistakes.*

    *Respond to children's questions with your own questions that encourage children to construct their own approaches to problems.*

    *Encourage multiple solutions. Children need to know that there are many possibilities and options.*

### Review the Activity

Ask participants to work in pairs or small groups to share and discuss their experiences teaching children to use problem-solving skills. Ask volunteers to summarize the lessons they learned from this activity. Record these tips on chart paper. Later, transcribe them and make copies to share with all participants.

### Offer Additional Resources and Activities

Provide poster board and markers for participants to make charts showing the five steps in the problem-solving process. Suggest that participants explain the process by analyzing the solution of a problem that actually came up in the classroom. They could highlight each step using photos, drawings, or other illustrations.

### End the Session

Offer to review and discuss the completed activity during individual meetings or phone conferences.

Introduce the next learning activity and the section, *Reflecting on Your Learning*.

# Learning Activity E

## Responding to Challenging Behavior

### Opening

Introduce the topic by asking questions such as the following:

- Why do we use the term *challenging behavior* instead of *bad behavior*?

- How do you respond to children who use behaviors such as kicking, swearing, and temper tantrums?

- Have you tried any of the suggestions in this learning activity? If so, what happened?

### Discuss the Text

Ask questions such as the following to encourage participants to share ideas:

- What challenging behaviors have children in your care used?

- What do you think the children were trying to express through their behavior?

- Have you considered any of the following reasons for a child's behavior?

  I don't feel well.

  I don't know what I'm supposed to do.

  I want you to notice me.

  I'm bored.

  I want more control.

  I'm scared.

  I'm frustrated.

- What was your immediate response? How did you help the child learn alternative ways to express his or her feelings or needs?

Form three small groups and assign each group one of the challenging behaviors discussed in the book: physical aggression, biting, or temper tantrums. Ask each group to read the section on the assigned behavior, talk about how they handle the problem in their program, and identify new strategies to try when the problem comes up again. Allow time for the groups to report the main points of their discussions.

## Review the Activity

Ask volunteers to discuss their experiences while completing this learning activity. To maintain confidentiality, remind participants not to use the child's name. Focus on identifying the cause of the challenging behavior and developing a plan to respond at home and at the program.

## Additional Resources and Activities

Invite a mental health specialist to share strategies for helping children whose challenging behavior interferes with their full participation in the program.

## Concluding the Module

### Reflecting on Your Learning

Return participants' completed activity forms and progress summaries with your comments. Offer to review and discuss these during individual meetings or phone conferences.

Ask participants to share something they learned while working on this module.

Ask participants to share some of the ways they adapted or changed their approach to guiding children's behavior. What have they done to minimize challenging behaviors? How have children reacted? How have families responded to the revised strategies?

Ask volunteers to share a few examples of curriculum connections related to guiding children's behavior.

Ask volunteers to share a few examples of strategies they used to build partnerships with families.

### End the Session

Schedule individual meetings with teachers to review their progress and schedule the knowledge and competency assessments.

# Chapter 4

# Chapter 4 (continued)

# Assessing Each Teacher's Progress

The *Caring for Preschool Children* training program includes two types of assessment for each module. *Knowledge Assessments* test a teacher's understanding of the information presented in the module. *Competency Assessments* require a teacher to apply knowledge and skills while working with children and families. For each module, the criteria for the competency assessment are drawn from the *Pre-Training Assessment*, and they are observable. Modules 1-12 include both knowledge and competency assessments. Module 13 has only a knowledge assessment because mastery of the skills developed through the module cannot be readily determined during an observation period.

This chapter describes the role of the trainer in the assessment process. It includes the *Knowledge Assessment* for each module, *Knowledge Assessment Answer Sheets* to facilitate scoring, and the *Competency Assessment* observation forms.

## The Assessment Process

Trainers administer the assessments after teachers have successfully completed all sections of a module: the *Overview*, the section on personal experiences, the *Pre-Training Assessment*, the learning activities, and *Reflecting on Your Learning*. During individual meetings, you meet with teachers to discuss their responses to the progress summary questions and review the strategies listed in the *Pre-Training Assessment* for the module. You discuss and jointly decide whether the teacher is ready for the assessments. (Having provided feedback on all the learning activities, you will already have a good idea whether an individual is ready.) If a teacher is not ready for assessment, you can suggest repeating one or more learning activities or provide additional training resources. If the decision is to proceed with the assessments, schedule times to administer them.

The assessment process is designed as another learning experience. If a teacher seems anxious, explain that continued support is available if his or her performance on either assessment is not successful. Reassure the individual that there will be additional opportunities to gain and demonstrate the necessary knowledge and skills.

Trainers will need to maintain a supply of the assessment forms, so it might be helpful to set up a filing system for storing copies of the *Knowledge Assessments* and *Competency Assessment* observation forms.

## Administering the Knowledge Assessments

The *Knowledge Assessments* are paper-and-pencil exercises that test knowledge of the information and concepts presented in the module. They are open-book tests because the intention is to validate what the teacher understands. The questions, which are based on the *Overview* and learning activities, include multiple-choice, matching, short-answer, and extended-answer formats. Most teachers will need approximately 20–30 minutes of uninterrupted time to complete each *Knowledge Assessment*. You may administer it before or after the *Competency Assessment* observation.

It may have been a long a time since some teachers have taken a test. Reassure them that the purpose is to validate how much they have learned about a topic. Remind them to read each question completely before attempting to answer it. Also suggest that they review all of their answers before turning in the assessment. This will help them catch mistakes such as writing on the wrong line or misreading a question.

## Conducting the Competency Assessments

The *Competency Assessment* observation forms are included at the end of this chapter. The form for each module includes a list of assessment criteria with spaces to indicate whether each criterion has been met, partially met, or not met. The *Competency Assessment* is scored on the basis of a scheduled, objective, systematic observation of a teacher while he or she works with children, as well as information you collected while working with the teacher on the module sections. The recommended observation period is one hour, but this will vary depending on the time of day, what the children are doing, and how often you have observed the teacher throughout the training program. You may want to observe at a particular time of day so you can witness a specific routine or activity (for example, you might want to observe arrival or departure times or outdoor play). For several modules, the competency assessment observation should be conducted at a specific time:

- Module 1, *Safe*, requires observation of an emergency drill.

- Module 11, *Families*, involves observation of drop-off or pick-up times.

- Module 12, *Program Management*, includes observation of a group of teachers planning together.

Read the criteria before the competency assessment observation and score any items that you can rate on the basis of your work with the teacher and previous observations of the teacher and the program environment. During the assessment observation, focus on the teacher's interactions with children, families, and other teachers. Take notes to document exactly what you see and hear so you can capture the teacher's interactions with and responses to children. Observation notes should provide objective descriptions of what you observed so you can share specific information with the teacher.

Useful observation notes are

- **Accurate:** Provide a factual and exact description of the teacher's and children's actions and language. Record what they do and say in the order in which they happen. Be specific. Try to include direct quotes whenever possible.

- **Objective:** Include only facts. Do not use labels, judgments, or inferences.

- **Complete:** Present a detailed picture of the setting, the number and ages of children, the teacher's actions and words, and the children's verbal and nonverbal responses. Describe the area in which the action took place and the materials and equipment in use. Include descriptions of activities from beginning to end.

Some of the competencies cannot be observed during the scheduled period. For these items, ask the teacher to show you any documents (e.g., portfolios of children's work, weekly planning forms, family communications) that demonstrate competence. You may also need to ask the teacher specific questions about particular items, such as established policies and procedures.

## Scoring the Assessments

Most adults are eager to know the results of their work. Score the assessments and share the results with the teacher as soon as possible.

The *Answer Sheets* indicate how to score each *Knowledge Assessment* question. When a question has more than one possible correct response, this is noted on the *Answer Sheets*. A perfect score is 100. A teacher must obtain a score of at least 80 percent.

Here is a sample of a completed *Competency Assessment* observation form for module 10, *Guidance*.

## 10 Guidance — Competency Assessment

**Teacher:** Ms. Kim          **Observer:** Ms. Sanchez

**Date/Time:** 5-4-04 / 10:00-11:30 AM          **Setting:** Central Preschool, Room 3

Review your records from this observation and other information you collected while this teacher was working on module 1. Score each criterion of competence that you can substantiate.

### Minimizing Problem Behavior and Encouraging Self-Discipline

**The competent teacher will:**          check the appropriate box — met / partially met / not met

1. Provide open-ended materials and activities that support varied interests and skills.          ☑ met

2. Establish a comfortable setting that looks and feels like children's homes.          ☑ met

3. Create cozy spaces where a child can be alone for awhile, yet still be visible to adults.          ☑ partially met

To score the *Competency Assessment*, review your notes from the assessment observation, previous observations, your examination of the environment, the teacher's documents, and, if applicable, your interview with the teacher. Use your notes to decide whether each criterion of competence was met, partially met, or not met. If you did not observe a criterion, leave the rating blank. A teacher should successfully meet most (80%) of the criteria.

## Sharing the Results

Schedule a meeting with the teacher to discuss the answers to the *Knowledge Assessment* and what you saw and heard during the *Competency Assessment* observation. Keep in mind that the purpose of the assessment process is to evaluate a teacher's understanding and application of the knowledge and skills presented in the module. In most cases, teachers already know whether they have mastered the needed knowledge and skills.

If the teacher has achieved a score of at least 80 percent on the *Knowledge Assessment*, offer your congratulations and briefly review any incorrect responses. If the teacher has not achieved a passing score, take your time going over the questions and answers so you can assess how much support the teacher needs to understand fully the material presented in the module. As stated earlier, the goal is to ensure competence and understanding, not simply to have the teacher pass the test. You might have the teacher repeat specific learning activities or read additional training resources.

Here is a possible approach to discussing the *Competency Assessment* results.

- **Begin by asking the teacher to comment on the observation period.** "Was today a typical day?" "Did everything go as you had planned?" "Were there any surprises?"

- **Discuss what went well and what problems existed, if any.** "What do you think went especially well?" "Is there anything you would want to do differently?"

- **Share your observation notes with the teacher.** "Let's look at my notes about what happened and see what we learn from them."

- **Review the criteria together.** Ask the teacher to assess which skills were clearly demonstrated and which were not.

- **Discuss your decision about the teacher's competence and explain the reasoning behind it.**

  If the teacher has clearly demonstrated competence, appears to understand the information, and applies it consistently while working with children, offer congratulations and take a few minutes to share observations of his or her progress.

  If the teacher has not met the criteria for competence, state your decision and explain why you think he or she needs more time to develop the necessary skills. Give examples from your observation notes. Ask what support would be most helpful and develop a plan to work together. Assure the teacher that the *Competency Assessment* may be rescored when his or her skills are stronger.

As teachers work on other modules, consider periodically reviewing their use of strategies from earlier modules. Your observations may sometimes indicate that a teacher needs to refresh knowledge and skills by reviewing learning activities already completed.

The following sections include copies of the *Knowledge Assessments, Answer Sheets* for all 13 modules, and the *Competency Assessment* observation forms for modules 1-12.

| Knowledge Assessment | Module 1: Safe |

*You may use* Caring for Preschool Children *and your* Skill-Building Journal *to complete this assessment.*

**Matching** (5 points each)

*Choose the lettered item in the right column that best matches each statement in the left column. Write the letter of your choice on the line next to the number of the statement.*

| | |
|---|---|
| ___ 1. Preschool children are curious and learn by exploring and using things. Sometimes they use materials in ways that adults do not intend. | (a) Using simple language, talk with children about dangerous situations and involve them in setting safety rules. Demonstrate the correct ways to use materials and equipment. While supervising, use positive statements as safety reminders. |
| ___ 2. Important aspects of a safe environment for children are providing adequate space for activities in each interest area and following guidelines that prevent or reduce injuries. | (b) Make sure all areas are continuously supervised. Know each child's abilities and personality, anticipate what he or she might do, and intervene when necessary. |
| ___ 3. Preschool children can understand and follow safety rules, although they need frequent reminders. | (c) Provide toys and materials that are durable and can withstand many uses. |
| ___ 4. Preschool children are ready to take short trips to nearby places of interest. | (d) Set up interest areas so children can move freely. Use low dividers so it is easy to see all children at all times. Create clear traffic paths so children do not get in each other's way. Place heavy toys on low shelves so children won't pull them down on themselves. |
| ___ 5. Preschool children are active learners. They like to run, climb, and jump, but they sometimes act without planning and before thinking about cause and effect. | (e) Minimize risks by teaching children how to walk safely near traffic and by following the program's procedures for safe trips. Plan ahead, anticipate potential problems, and take safety precautions. |

**Fill in the Blank** (5 points each)

*Complete each sentence. Number 7 requires two answers, worth a total of 10 points.*

6. If you know or suspect that a child has been poisoned, immediately_____

_____.

7. Two important rules to remember when giving first aid are

 a._____.

 b._____.

8. When checking a child for injuries, start your examination with the child's _____.

**Short Answer** (5 points each)

*Complete the following exercises. Number 12 requires two answers, worth a total of 10 points.*

9.  Restate the following rule as a positive statement: *Do not climb on the table.*

10. Give an example of a safety precaution adults can model for children.

11. Explain what you would do if a child continued to break a safety rule.

12. State **two** safety reasons why the daily schedule should include time for both vigorous play and quiet activities.

a.

b.

**Multiple Choice** (5 points each)

*Check the response that best completes each sentence.*

13. One of the ways to prevent injuries is for teachers to

   ☐ a. make sure that children never take risks.
   ☐ b. make sure all areas and activities are continually supervised.
   ☐ c. divide the children into groups of boys and girls.
   ☐ d. let children explore cause and effect by bumping into each other's tricycles.

14. When teachers talk with young children about safety, they use all of the following strategies *except*

   ☐ a. using open-ended prompts to help children think about ways to stay safe.
   ☐ b. reassuring the children that the program is a safe place and they will be protected.
   ☐ c. explaining and demonstrating the safe way to use materials, play games, and carry out routines.
   ☐ d. making children fearful so they will never forget the rules.

**Extended Answer** (10 points each)

*Complete the following exercises.*

15. Explain why it is important to involve children in setting a few simple classroom rules.

16. Describe a child whose behavior makes it necessary to provide extra support on trips away from the program, and explain how you would provide that support.

## Knowledge Assessment    Module 2: Healthy

*You may use* Caring for Preschool Children *and your* Skill-Building Journal *to complete this assessment.*

### Matching (5 points each)

*Choose the lettered item in the right column that best matches each statement in the left column. Write the letter of your choice on the line next to the number of the statement.*

| | |
|---|---|
| ___ 1. Germs can be passed from one person to another. | (a) Ill children need additional rest, appropriate food and drinks, close supervision and comfort, and sometimes medication. |
| ___ 2. Some children have repeated non-accidental injuries or offer behavioral clues that teachers should notice. | (b) Teachers serve a variety of healthy foods for snacks and meals; share relaxed, family-style meals; taste all the foods served and encourage children to do the same; take water breaks throughout the day; offer cooking activities; tend a vegetable garden; and offer books about nutrition. |
| ___ 3. Children learn good health habits through routines. | (c) Teachers follow universal precautions—handwashing, cleaning and disinfecting, and using gloves for contact with body fluids—to prevent the spread of diseases. As appropriate, they also encourage children to follow these precautions. |
| ___ 4. Sick children who remain at the center need extra attention. | (d) Teachers learn to recognize the signs of possible child abuse and neglect and report suspected cases as required by state and local laws. |
| ___ 5. Preschool children can learn about good nutrition. | (e) Teachers help children practice healthy habits daily. They encourage regular toothbrushing, frequent handwashing, using and discarding tissues, and careful food handling. Children are encouraged to do as much as possible for themselves and are invited to help maintain a healthy environment. |

### Fill in the Blank (5 points each)

*Complete each sentence. Number 7 requires two answers, worth a total of 10 points.*

6. The HIV attacks the immune system that protects the body from viruses and bacteria. It can be transmitted in the following ways: _____

_____

_____

_____

_____.

7. Two reasons why cooking activities are good learning opportunities for preschool children are

   a._____.

   b._____.

8. A mandated reporter of possible child abuse and neglect is a person who_____

   _____.

## Short Answer (5 points each)

*Complete the following exercises.*

9. Describe one aspect of family-style dining.

10. Explain why teachers wash their own hands and help as children wash their hands thoroughly and frequently.

11. Give a specific example of how health and nutrition learning can be incorporated into a daily classroom routine or interest area activity.

## Multiple Choice (5 points each)

*Check the response that best completes each sentence.*

12. An example of emotional child abuse is

    ☐ a. when a child is allowed to make choices.
    ☐ b. when a child has a hard time sharing and likes to play alone.
    ☐ c. when a parent teases her child because she is overweight.
    ☐ d. when a child cries because his friend may not come home with him every day.

13. A common risk factor for families that can lead to child abuse and neglect is
    ☐ a. not having two parents living in the same household.
    ☐ b. having children under the age of five.
    ☐ c. having children who continually test behavioral limits.
    ☐ d. being under a lot of continuous stress.

14. During lunch, teachers can help make the meal relaxed and pleasant for children by

    ☐ a. making sure children eat everything on their plates.
    ☐ b. allowing a few children to eat at the table at a time.
    ☐ c. asking children to take a deep breath before eating; keeping a calm and leisurely pace during the meal.
    ☐ d. playing lively marching music while everyone is eating.

15. If there is an outbreak of head lice in your program,

☐   a. throw out all stuffed animals and pillows.
☐   b. explain that the children are not bathing often enough.
☐   c. share information with families about the life cycle of lice and steps that must be taken at home and at the program.
☐   d. call a pest control company and make sure that families know the program will be closed when insecticides are sprayed.

## Extended Answer (10 points each)

*Complete the following exercises.*

16. Discuss how teachers promote wellness by sanitizing indoor program spaces. In your answer, include information about what should be cleaned and how.

17. Discuss the key role teachers play in preventing and stopping child abuse and neglect. In your answer, explain why they are in a position to notice signs of possible abuse and neglect and the importance of reporting what they notice.

| Knowledge Assessment | Module 3: Learning Environment |
|---|---|

*You may use* Caring for Preschool Children *and your* Skill-Building Journal *to complete this assessment.*

## Matching (5 points each)

*Choose the lettered item in the right column that best matches each statement in the left column. Write the letter of your choice on the line next to the number of the statement.*

| | |
|---|---|
| ___ 1. Preschool children enjoy challenges and are eager to try new things. They have many ideas about what to do and how to do it. | (a) Divide the room into smaller spaces. Limit the number of children who may be in an area at the same time. Clearly define areas for quiet activities, such as reading and art, as well as areas for more active play, such as dramatic play and block building. |
| ___ 2. Preschool children can express their feelings in many ways. | (b) Provide a rich variety of open-ended materials, equipment, and activities to encourage different kinds of exploration. Arrange opportunities for children to work independently and with others, and to take responsibility for maintaining the classroom environment. |
| ___ 3. Preschool children have lots of energy and want to gain physical skills. They like to practice skills and do things again and again. | (c) Develop a daily schedule that provides a balance of activities for children. Illustrate the schedule and post it in the room so children can learn the order of daily events. |
| ___ 4. Preschool children learn best in small groups and when they are offered clear choices. | (d) Provide lots of writing and drawing materials, such as crayons, markers, paints, paper so that children can draw pictures and represent their ideas. Encourage children to act out their life experiences and express in the dramatic play and other interest areas. |
| ___ 5. Preschool children like structure and routines. When the schedule is the same each day, they learn to predict what will happen and what to expect. | (e) Provide opportunities for children to develop their large and small muscle skills. Repeat activities so children can practice, master skills, and experience success. |

## Fill in the Blank (5 points each)

*Complete each sentence. Number 7 requires two answers, worth a total of 10 points.*

6. Transitions are _____.

7. Two reasons to include a variety of separate interest areas in preschool classrooms are to

_____ and

_____.

8. It is recommended that children have at least _____ minutes of outdoor play every day in full-day programs.

9. Outdoor space should be organized by _____.

## Short Answer (5 points each)

*Complete the following exercises.*

10. Give an example of how outdoor activities or equipment can be adapted for a child with a disability.

11. Choose one interest area and briefly explain how it should be arranged to support children's learning.

## Multiple Choice (5 points each)

*Check the response that best completes each sentence.*

12. It is important to plan for transitions so that

   ☐ a. children will not be bored and restless.
   ☐ b. children will not fall asleep before nap time.
   ☐ c. children will not start a new activity until it is explained.
   ☐ d. teachers will not feel badly about hurrying children who are too slow.

13. An ideal outdoor program environment should include

   ☐ a. a nearby pond.
   ☐ b. sunny and shady areas.
   ☐ c. access from the neighborhood.
   ☐ d. a view of the highway.

14. An appropriate daily schedule for preschool children should

   ☐ a. ensure that children use the toilet at the same time every day.
   ☐ d. include time for language drills.
   ☐ e. limit outdoor time in cold weather.
   ☐ f. offer a balance of active and quiet times, and child-initiated and teacher-directed activities.

15. An appropriate activity for children in the Discovery Area is

   ☐ a. organizing a marching band.
   ☐ b. observing and categorizing.
   ☐ c. riding bikes.
   ☐ d. jumping off a table to test a parachute.

**Extended Answer** (10 points each)

*Complete the following exercises.*

16. Explain why it is important to include large blocks of choice time and a variety of activity choices in the daily schedule.

17. Describe what teachers can do to make transitions run smoothly.

| Knowledge Assessment | Module 4: Physical |
|---|---|

*You may use* Caring for Preschool Children *and your* Skill-Building Journal *to complete this assessment.*

## Matching (5 points each)

*Choose the lettered item in the right column that best matches each statement in the left column. Write the letter of your choice on the line next to the number of the statement.*

| | |
|---|---|
| __ 1. Three-year-old children are typically gaining more control over using their fingers, hands, and wrists. | (a) Encourage children's self-help skills, such as pulling pants, eating with utensils, putting on shoes, and washing hands. Provide many opportunities to practice small-muscle skills. |
| __ 2. Four-year-old children have more refined small-muscle control and hand-eye coordination than 3-year olds. | (b) Offer children physical challenges without causing frustration. Allow them to practice their skills and share their joy as they improve their abilities. Do not interrupt or correct their attempts, unless safety is a concern. |
| __ 3. Most 5-year-old children can run fast, climb freely, and enjoy ball games. | (c) Provide smaller versions of the materials children used when they were younger, such as Legos, beads and strings, and pegs and pegboards. |
| __ 4. Preschool children vary in their development of physical skills. Children of the same age can be at different levels of physical skill. | (d) Help older children begin learning skills to play sports and games. |
| __ 5. Physical development is related to children's self-esteem. Children feel increasingly competent as they learn to control their bodies. | (e) Offer open-ended materials and equipment that can be used in different ways by children of different skill levels. |

## Fill in the Blank (5 points each)

*Complete each sentence. Number 7 requires three answers, worth a total of 15 points.*

6. A cue is a _____.

7. **Three** ways to offer cues are by _____,

_____, and

_____.

8. The best way to know and understand how individual children use their fine and gross motor skills is by

_____.

**Short Answer** (5 points each)

*Complete each exercise.*

9. Give an example of a cue for a child who is learning to swing.

10. Explain how children practice their fine motor skills in the Sand and Water Area.

11. Explain how children practice their gross motor skills through Music and Movement activities.

12. Identify an open-ended material or piece of equipment and explain how children of different physical skill levels can use it.

**Multiple Choice** (5 points each)

*Check the response that best completes each sentence.*

13. When teachers encourage children to practice a skill, they are

    ☐ a. making sure children are performing at their expected level.
    ☐ b. helping children develop feelings of competence.
    ☐ c. following the program's guidelines.
    ☐ d. showing them how to keep safe.

14. When teachers offer cues to children, they are

    ☐ a. making sure children learn how to do a task correctly.
    ☐ b. formally assessing the child's ability.
    ☐ c. helping children focus attention on their actions.
    ☐ d. helping children learn to listen.

**Extended Answer** (10 points each)

*Complete the following exercises.*

15. Explain how physical development is connected to **two** other areas of development (cognitive, emotional, social, or language).

16. Choose one general physical skill and describe the continuum of development for that skill.

| Knowledge Assessment | Module 5: Cognitive |

*You may use* Caring for Preschool Children *and your* Skill-Building Journal *to complete this assessment.*

## Matching (5 points each)

*Choose the lettered item in the right column that best matches each statement in the left column. Write the letter of your choice on the line next to the number of the statement.*

| | |
|---|---|
| __ 1. Preschool children use all of their senses—smell, taste, touch, sight, and hearing—to explore and investigate. | (a) Listen carefully to children's questions and ask questions to find out what they really want to know. Give answers they can understand. Ask questions to stretch their thinking. Model ways to use books and other resources to find answers. Encourage children to think of many possible answers or solutions. |
| __ 2. Preschool children are interested in cause and effect (what makes things happen). | (b) Ask questions to help children understand how past experiences relate to what is happening now. Build on children's interests and extend their ideas. Help children apply what they have learned to new situations. |
| __ 3. Preschool children believe there is a purpose for everything and ask many questions: *What? Why? How?* | (c) Provide a variety of appealing table toys and interesting materials that can be organized in different ways, such as rocks, shells, buttons, and keys. Comment on and ask children to talk about what they are doing. |
| __ 4. Preschool children construct understanding by making connections between new experiences and ideas and what they already know. | (d) Provide a rich variety of open-ended materials, equipment, and objects to inspire children to explore in different ways. |
| __ 5. Preschool children can match, sort, classify, and compare objects. | (e) Set up activities and provide materials that allow children to test their ideas. Provide objects for children to take apart and examine, and tools they can use to explore and investigate. Ask questions that encourage children to make predictions. |

## Fill in the Blank (5 points each)

*Complete each sentence. Number 7 requires two answers, worth a total of 10 points.*

6. Cognitive development is _____.

7. Teachers ask children questions in order to _____

   and_____.

8. An open-ended question is one that _____.

**Short Answer** (5 points each)

*Complete the following exercises. Number 12 requires two answers, worth a total of 10 points*

9. Give an example of a question that helps children think about cause and effect.

10. Give an example of a question that encourages children to make a prediction.

11. Give an example of a closed question.

12. Identify and briefly define **two** areas of mathematics that preschool children should explore. *(A and b are each worth 2.5 points.)*

a.

b.

**Multiple Choice** (5 points each)

*Check the response that best completes each sentence.*

13. The first step in planning a study is to

☐ a. develop safety rules for neighborhood walks.
☐ b. take photographs of children's woodworking projects.
☐ c. identify a good topic.
☐ d. invite families to watch a play that the children perform.

14. When a child serves a cracker to each person in the class, she is constructing an understanding of

☐ a. measurement.
☐ b. how to make friends.
☐ c. snack time.
☐ d. one-to-one correspondence.

15. Listening to what children say is an excellent way to learn

  ☐ a. whether they are ready for formal assessments.
  ☐ b. how they think and try to make sense of their world.
  ☐ c. whether they have good hearing.
  ☐ d. whether they are developing gross motor skills.

**Extended Answer** (10 points each)

*Complete the following exercises.*

16. Explain how cognitive development is related to **two** other areas of development (physical, emotional, social, or language development).

a.

b.

17. Explain why it is important to encourage children to explore, investigate, make discoveries, and solve problems both on their own and with other children.

## Knowledge Assessment                    Module 6: Communication

*You may use* Caring for Preschool Children *and your* Skill-Building Journal *to complete this assessment.*

### Matching (5 points each)

*Choose the lettered item in the right column that best matches each statement in the left column. Write the letter of your choice on the line next to the number of the statement.*

| | |
|---|---|
| __ 1. Preschool children use language to construct understandings about their life experiences. | (a) Model standard language when speaking with other adults and with children. Use opportunities such as circle time to encourage children to practice conversational skills such as taking turns, asking questions, and waiting for a response. |
| __ 2. In order to become readers and writers, children need to develop phonological awareness. | (b) Display a variety of print that is related to what is going on in the classroom and activity areas. Use words and pictures to label shelves and storage containers. |
| __ 3. Children learn to be partners in conversations with much practice and gradually over time. | (c) Learn some basic words of the children's home languages and use them in the classroom. When speaking English, talk slowly and clearly, pausing longer than usual at natural breaks. Use gestures, pictures, and objects as cues while you talk. Repeat words that are important to the meaning of what you are saying. |
| __ 4. Children who hear language and see written words in meaningful contexts develop an understanding that spoken and written languages are related. | (d) Provide dramatic play props that encourage children to listen and speak as they act out roles. Introduce new vocabulary and concepts that expand their thinking and talking. Read aloud and talk about story characters, settings, and plots, and help children relate stories to their own lives. |
| __ 5. It is important for teachers to support children who are learning English as a second language. | (e) Call children's attention to sounds and rhymes when singing, reciting finger plays, and reading simple poems. Omit the last word that rhymes in a familiar story so children can predict it. Point out the initial sounds of words, and clap out syllables. |

### Fill in the Blank (5 points each)

*Complete each sentence. Number 6 requires two answers, worth a total of 10 points.*

6. Preschool children typically use language to _____ and

   _____.

7. One way to extend children's interest in a read-aloud book is _____

   _____.

8. One reason teachers run their finger under the text as they read aloud is

   _____.

9. One reason why teachers let children watch them write and tell them what they are writing is

   _____.

## Short Answer (5 points each)

*Complete the following exercises. Number 12 requires two answers, worth a total of 10 points.*

10. Give an example of a strategy to use when reading aloud to children.

11. Give an example of a warning sign that a preschool child may have a language delay or disability and may need an assessment by a speech and language specialist.

12. List two ways, other than books, that teachers can include meaningful print in their classrooms or outdoors.

a.

b.

## Multiple Choice (5 points each)

*Check the response that best completes each sentence or that is the best example.*

13. In a program that promotes children's communication skills,

   ☐ a. teachers use only words that they are sure the children already know.
   ☐ b. teachers ask open-ended questions that encourage children to think.
   ☐ c. there many children and staff members in the classroom.
   ☐ d. teachers correct children when they mispronounce words.

14. The following is an example of a question that engages children in conversation.

   ☐ a. "Did you like your ice cream?"
   ☐ b. "What kinds of tricks did the magician do?"
   ☐ c. "What color is the sun?"
   ☐ d. "Will you put the blocks back in the bin?"

**Extended Answer** (10 points each)

*Complete the following exercises.*

15. Select five interest areas. List literacy materials you would provide in each area and explain why you would include them there.

16. *Briefly* explain five ways in which teachers use the environment to encourage children to speak and listen.

## Knowledge Assessment                                    Module 7: Creative

*You may use* Caring for Preschool Children *and your* Skill-Building Journal *to complete this assessment.*

### Matching (5 points each)

*Choose the lettered item in the right column that best matches each statement in the left column. Write the letter of your choice on the line next to the number of the statement.*

| | |
|---|---|
| __ 1. Preschool children become completely absorbed in an engaging activity and stay involved as long as their interest lasts. | (a) Provide dramatic play props that encourage children to listen and speak as they act out roles. Introduce new vocabulary and concepts that expand their thinking and conversation. Read and talk about story characters, settings, and plots, and help children relate them to their own lives. |
| __ 2. Music is a great way to promote children's self-expression. Children respond to music at an early age and enjoy moving rhythmically when listening to music. | (b) Plan a schedule with large blocks of choice time, and offer a balance of activity choices. Adapt the schedule, when appropriate, so children have enough time to act on their ideas. |
| __ 3. Preschool children tend to enjoy the creative process more than the products they make. They enjoy exploring different materials, using their bodies, and mixing things together. | (c) Provide opportunities for children to explore and investigate and to use information and their imaginations. Ask questions to help children describe what they are doing and to relate new experiences to what they already know. |
| __ 4. Preschool children use language to understand their life experiences. | (d) Offer a variety of open-ended art materials, such as clay, playdough, paints, poster board, scrap materials, paste. |
| __ 5. Preschool children's cognitive development is connected to their creativity. When teachers encourage children to solve problems and think in new ways, children construct understandings about the world. | (e) Play singing games, play music during transition times, have a variety of rhythm instruments in the music and movement activity area for children to use. |

### Fill in the Blank (5 points each)

*Complete each sentence. Number 6 requires two answers, worth a total of 10 points. Number 8 requires three answers, worth a total of 15 points.*

6. Two reasons to provide painting and drawing opportunities and materials for preschool children are

    a._____.

    b._____.

7. A collage is _____.

8. Three characteristics of preschool children that are related to creativity are

   a._____.

   b._____.

   c._____.

## Short Answer (5 points each)

*Complete the following exercises.*

9. Give an example of a question that encourages creative thinking.

10. Name one of the developmental stages of children's art and briefly explain what children do during that stage.

11. List at least two characteristics of good songs to sing with preschool children.

## Multiple Choice (5 points each)

*Check the response that best completes each sentence.*

12 Music and movement activities encourage self-expression and

   ☐  a. help children explore ways to move their bodies.
   ☐  b. help teachers get a break during the day.
   ☐  c. help teachers learn which children have rhythm.
   ☐  d. help children learn the latest dances.

13. When families share their favorite songs with the class, they give teachers is a good opportunity to

   ☐  a. help children learn about different cultures and languages.
   ☐  b. seek out talent for the program's talent show.
   ☐  c. use the time to do important paperwork.
   ☐  d. help families learn to sing better.

**Extended Answer** (10 points each)

*Complete the following exercises.*

14. Explain how teachers convey their enthusiasm and respect for children's ideas and imaginations.

15. Describe how you would guide children through their first painting experience. Explain what you would say and do, as well as the materials you would provide.

| Knowledge Assessment | Module 8: Self |
|---|---|

*You may use* Caring for Preschool Children *and your* Skill-Building Journal *to complete this assessment.*

## Matching (5 points each)

*Choose the lettered item in the right column that best matches each statement in the left column. Write the letter of your choice on the line next to the number of the statement.*

| | |
|---|---|
| __ 1. Preschool children learn about themselves through interactions with peers and adults. | (a) Consider both developmental and individual characteristics of each child when purchasing materials and organizing activities. Provide a wide variety of open-ended materials for different interests and skill levels. Arrange interest areas and plan activities so that all children can participate. |
| __ 2. Preschool children have a wide range of interests and abilities. | (b) When talking to and listening to children, position yourself at their eye level. Encourage children to talk about their feelings and take their concerns seriously. Listen for messages underlying what they say. |
| __ 3. Preschool children learn new things and gain a greater understanding of themselves and the world everyday. As they master new skills, children come to see themselves as capable and competent. | (c) Provide many opportunities for children to interact with each other throughout the day. Model appropriate language and behavior and intervene in children's interactions only when necessary. |
| __ 4. It is important to listen and respond to children respectfully. Sometimes children's language doesn't express their feelings. | (d) Give permission to a child who is inattentive to move around or change activities. Model language to help children recognize and verbalize their feelings. For example, you might respond to a squirming child, "You seem a little restless, Jason. Do you want to help me pass out the cookies?" |
| __ 5. Children's behavior can also be a way to ask for attention and encouragement. It is important to interpret children's behavior and body language as well as what they say. | (e) Provide many opportunities for children to do things independently, as well as opportunities for children to work together. Plan a schedule with long blocks of time when children can choose what they want to do and with whom. Accept mistakes as a natural part of learning. |

## Fill in the Blank (5 points each)

*Complete each sentence. Question 8 requires two answers, worth a total of 10 points.*

6. *Sense of self* is defined as_____.

7. In addition to giving all interested children a chance to participate, it is important to repeat activities so that

_____.

8. In addition to skills and developmental levels, children are different from each other in other ways, including temperament and personality. Two personality traits that might differ are

_____ and _____.

9. One of the hardest things for teachers to know is when to offer a child help and when to

_____.

10. It is important for teachers to talk with children about their families during the day because

_____

_____.

## Short Answer (5 points each)

*Complete the following exercises.*

11. Name one of the first three stages of social/emotional development that Eric Erikson describes and briefly state what children do and learn during that stage.

12. Why is it important for teachers to listen when children express their feelings?

13. Why do teachers invite children to help with meaningful jobs in the classroom?

## Multiple Choice (5 points each)

*Check the response that best completes each sentence.*

14. The best way for teachers to recognize children's efforts and accomplishments is by

   ☐ a. making thoughtful and specific comments about what they are doing and what they have achieved.
   ☐ b. offering activities that are very easy so children never become frustrated.
   ☐ c. giving them a lot of praise.
   ☐ d. comparing their efforts to others so they can know how they are doing.

15. An example of a personalized morning greeting is,

   ☐ a. "Good morning. Come on in!"
   ☐ b. "Hello. How are you today?"
   ☐ c. "Amad, I see you brought your favorite book with you today. Would you like me to read it at story time?"
   ☐ d. "Come on in. Let's hurry and sit down."

**Extended Answer** (10 points each)

*Complete the following exercises.*

16. Describe one way teachers can get to know and appreciate each child as an individual.

17. Explain how the development of a child's sense of self is connected to language development.

| Knowledge Assessment | Module 9: Social |
|---|---|

*You may use Caring for Preschool Children and your Skill-Building Journal to complete this assessment.*

## Matching (5 points each)

*Choose the lettered item in the right column that best matches each statement in the left column. Write the letter of your choice on the line next to the number of the statement.*

| | |
|---|---|
| ___ 1. Preschool children develop and practice social skills during play. | (a) Create dramatic play settings by making a variety of materials and props available both indoors and outdoors. Expand children's knowledge of potential play scenarios. Join children's play by following their lead and assuming a role. |
| ___ 2. Children feel comfortable in a classroom that functions as a community, with a supportive program that responds to individual and group needs. | (b) Plan group activities that promote children's sense of belonging, and give children meaningful classroom jobs. Read and discuss books about feelings, friendship, and being helpful. Involve children in setting classroom rules, and hold daily class meetings for children to share ideas, discuss feelings, and solve problems. |
| ___ 3. Dramatic play helps children explore roles and make sense of the world. They share ideas and knowledge, converse with one another, and learn to negotiate and compromise. | (c) Provide many opportunities for children to cooperate, take turns, share ideas, and help others. Arrange the environment so that small groups of children can work together. Include interesting materials that can be used by children with different skills. |
| ___ 4. Preschool children develop caring behavior over a long period. The most direct way for children to learn caring behavior is by watching and listening to adults who care for them. | (d) Establish a classroom rule that no child is allowed to tell another child that he or she may not play. Create opportunities for children to play together and help them join activities if they have difficulty doing so. Pair children to work together on meaningful tasks. |
| ___ 5. Children need to learn how to make friends. Some children have difficulty making friends because they are shy, aggressive, or rejected by their peers for other reasons. | (e) Use each child's name often, and position yourself at the child's eye level when you are conversing. Share ideas and feelings, ask questions, make positive comments, and have friendly conversations. Control of strong feelings and cooperate with families and colleagues. Take and share photos of daily and special activities, to celebrate both individuals and the group. |

## Fill in the Blank (5 points each)

*Complete each sentence.*

6. It is important to provide a balance between structured and unstructured activities because _____

_____

_____.

7. A *prop box* is_____
   _____.

8. It is important to announce _____
   in advance so children can finish what they are doing and prepare themselves to begin another activity.

9. Children's play evolves in three stages: solitary play, parallel play, and cooperative play. When children organize their own activities, assign roles, make up rules, assign specific tasks, and work toward a common goal, their play is_____.

10. Children need to understand their own feelings in order to figure out how to get along with others. One way teachers help children understand their own feelings is_____
    _____.

## Short Answer (5 points each)

*Complete the following exercises.*

11. Explain one strategy teachers use to support children's efforts to make and keep friends.

12. Give one example of how daily routines help children develop social skills. (*Use a strategy that is different from the one you explained in question 10.*)

13. Why is it important for teachers to overcome their negative feelings about children who are overly aggressive or disruptive?

14. Briefly explain one strategy teachers use to help children learn to take turns.

## Multiple Choice (5 points each)

*Check the response that best completes each sentence.*

15. When a very shy child is playing with a collection alone, the teacher could help the child feel secure by saying,

    ☐ a. "Why don't you find someone to play with?"
    ☐ b. "Go play with Carla."
    ☐ c. "I see you made an interesting design with the buttons."
    ☐ d. "Don't you like the other children?"

16. When children play alongside each other and sometimes talk together, that is called

☐ a. social play.
☐ b. parallel play.
☐ c. imitation play.
☐ d. free play.

**Extended Answer** (10 points each)

*Complete the following exercises.*

17. Describe two strategies that teachers use to guide and extend children's play together.

18. Explain two ways to promote the social development of children who yell and push when they are angry.

| **Knowledge Assessment** | **Module 10: Guidance** |

*You may use* Caring for Preschool Children *and your* Skill-Building Journal *to complete this assessment.*

## Matching (5 points each)

*Choose the lettered item in the right column that best matches each statement in the left column. Write the letter of your choice on the line next to the number of the statement.*

| | |
|---|---|
| ___ 1. Preschool children like to play with others and are still learning to share and take turns. | (a) Establish a few important classroom rules. Have the children help set them. Make sure the rules are clear, positive, and help children understand what they are supposed to do. |
| ___ 2. Helping children develop self-discipline is important. Over time, teachers guide and direct children toward independent choices, balancing their needs with those of others, accepting responsibility for their actions, and delaying gratification. | (b) Provide opportunities for children to work together to solve problems themselves. Ask open-ended questions to encourage multiple approaches and solutions. Give children time to respond and accept mistakes as a natural part of the learning process. |
| ___ 3. Children are more likely to follow rules if they know the reasons for them and help to create them. | (c) Regularly exchange information with families about how their children are developing and learning. Describe any behaviors that are of concern and discuss strategies to support the child. Address the behavior, not the child, as challenging. |
| ___ 4. Children who see themselves as problem solvers are more likely to be able to tackle difficult problems as they get older. | (d) Model appropriate behavior and language at all times. Help children identify and express their ideas and feelings constructively. |
| ___ 5. It is best for teachers and families to work together to help children with challenging behavior. | (e) Provide duplicates of popular toys and order enough consumable materials for the group. Offer activities more than once so all interested children can participate. Set up a turn-taking system for interest areas. |

## Fill in the Blank (5 points each)

*Complete each sentence. Number 7 requires two answers, worth a total of 10 points.*

6. Discipline is often confused with _____.

7. Effective guidance techniques are based on the _____

   and _____ characteristics of children.

8. Teachers assume a firm, authoritative role only when necessary to_____.

9. Preschool children can move their bodies in many ways and sometimes do not think about

   _____.

## Short Answer (5 points each)

*Complete each exercise. Number 12 requires **three** answers, worth a total of 15 points.*

10. Give an example of how teachers support children who seem to have difficulty paying attention.

11. Give an example of how teachers can promote social problem-solving skills in the classroom.

12. Identify **three** possible causes for a child's challenging behavior.

a.

b.

c.

## Multiple Choice (5 points each)

*Check the item that is the best example, response, or step.*

13. An example of providing positive guidance is

☐ a. making a child sit still for at least 25 minutes.
☐ b. helping a child recite all the classroom rules from memory.
☐ c. keeping directions simple and clear and using simple, positive reminders.
☐ d. invite families to punish children who misbehave at the program.

14. Which of the following responses will help a child to develop self-discipline?

☐ a. "Stop that, Joseph. You know you're not supposed to push."
☐ b. "You seem to need some time alone, Vita. Try reading a book in the Library Area."
☐ c. "If you had sense, you'd stop rocking that chair on two legs."
☐ d. "You'll miss recess if you don't listen to what I tell you."

15. Which of the following is a problem-solving step?

☐ a. Defining the problem.
☐ b. Setting a deadline.
☐ c. Ignoring the problem for a little while.
☐ d. Convincing another person to see the situation your way.

## Extended Answer (10 points)

16. Explain at least two strategies to support a child who is frustrated by an activity.

## Knowledge Assessment       Module 11: Families

*You may use* Caring for Preschool Children *and your* Skill-Building Journal *to complete this assessment.*

### Matching (5 points each)

*Choose the lettered item in the right column that best matches each statement in the left column. Write the letter of your choice on the line next to the number of the statement.*

| | |
|---|---|
| __ 1. Partnerships between families and teachers are extremely important for everyone. Children feel secure knowing that their families and teachers work together to keep them safe and help them to learn. | (a) Explain to families the importance of letting children know when they are leaving the program and to assure them that they will return to pick them up. |
| __ 2. Separation difficulties are stressful for children and families. Teachers can provide guidance to help them with the separation process. | (b) Invite families to be part of the program's activities. Invite families to visit or to help in the classroom, come along on study trips, share special events, and contribute to supplies and projects. |
| __ 3. Keeping families informed is crucial to successful partnerships between families and the program. Teachers use many approaches to exchange information with families. | (c) Hold conferences throughout the year and make sure families know they can ask for a conference whenever they want one. Keep families informed daily and throughout the year about how their children are developing and learning. |
| __ 4. Most families want to be involved in their children's lives in the program. Family involvement and support can be an important resource for the program. | (d) Get to know a little about each family. Communicate frequently to share information and offer a variety of ways for families to participate in the program. Plan and hold conferences, and provide support to families in a variety of ways. |
| __ 5. Conferences are opportunities for teachers to focus on one child and family. Through conferences, families and teachers share information about how best to support an individual child's development and learning. | (e) Find ways to communicate with families regularly. Ask families which methods would be most useful to them. Use newsletters, e-mail, conferences, special events, phone calls, and informal conversations to keep families informed about their children and program. |

### Fill in the Blank (5 points each)

*Complete each sentence.*

6. In addition to sharing information about their children, families can share _____

   _____.

7. Families should not leave the program without saying _____ to their children.

8. It is helpful to provide families with a copy of the program's _____

   _____.

9. Teachers should be aware of _____ differences that need to be recognized and respected.

## Short Answer (5 points each)

*Complete the following exercises.*

10. Explain what is meant by the term, *maintaining confidentiality.*

11. Give an example of information about a child that a teacher will want to learn from the family during a conference.

12. Give an example of information about their child that a family will want to learn from the teacher during a conference.

13. Identify a source of long-term family stress.

14. Give an example of how teachers help families find resources or get more information about a topic that interests them.

## Multiple Choice (5 points each)

*Check the response that best completes each sentence.*

15. A way teachers can make family conferences successful is to

   ☐ a. give families a lot of materials to read and study ahead of time.
   ☐ b. repeat what they think they've heard to make sure they understand what a family member said.
   ☐ c. make sure families arrive on time.
   ☐ d. hold conferences early in the morning when everyone is fresh.

16. If there is a conflict between the program and a family's expectations, a teacher may want to

   ☐ a. ask the program director to request the family's cooperation.
   ☐ b. tell the family that the program has specific guidelines they must follow.
   ☐ c. ignore the problem until the parent comes to accept the program.
   ☐ d. try to understand the family's view and jointly determine a solution.

**Extended Answer** (10 points each)

*Complete the following exercises.*

17. Explain how you would prepare for a conference with a family. Discuss your ideas about scheduling the conference, as well as the information you would want to gather.

18. Describe one way to involve families in a specific activity and how teachers ensure that their participation is meaningful for them.

## Knowledge Assessment    Module 12: Program Management

*You may use* Caring for Preschool Children *and your* Skill-Building Journal *to complete this assessment.*

**Matching** (5 points each)

*Choose the lettered item in the right column that best matches each statement in the left column. Write the letter of your choice on the line next to the number of the statement.*

| | |
|---|---|
| __ 1. Program management includes creating a supportive learning environment, guiding children's learning, and assessing children's progress. Knowledge of children's developmental and individual characteristics guides program planning and implementation. | (a) Provide activities that accommodate the varying skills, interests, and abilities of all children. Make changes or adjustments for individual children, as needed for them to participate in all parts of the program. Make inclusion an integral part of the program's environment and practice. |
| __ 2. Portfolios are a great way to use samples of children's work to document their progress over time. A portfolio includes concrete examples of a child's efforts, achievements, and learning style. | (b) High-quality programs are based on child development principles and theory, and they are tailored to correspond with the characteristics of individual children. Work as a team to plan and implement a responsive program. Appreciate and use the strengths of all team members, including teachers, families, and volunteers. |
| __ 3. Individual needs can be met in group activities, as well as by working with children one-on-one. | (c) Collect examples of children's work throughout the year. Document and keep observation notes about what children do. Organize examples that show how the child learns and is progressing. Invite families to contribute, and share the collection with family members and their children. |
| __ 4. High quality programs ensure that every child can learn and succeed. An environment that supports inclusion of children with disabilities and different needs helps all children to thrive. | (d) Ask different types of questions so that children with different cognitive and language skills can participate in group discussions. Offer encouragement and open-ended materials and activities that allow children to develop their own approaches to tasks. |

**Fill in the Blank** (5 points each)

*Complete each sentence. Numbers 6 and 7 each require two answers, so each question is worth a total of 10 points.*

5. Useful observation notes are complete, accurate, and_____.

6. A program should have a written _____ to guide teachers' work and an

_____ to determine how each child is progressing.

7. Two reasons why teachers observe children are

    a._____.

    b._____.

8. It important to observe children in different settings and at different times of the day because_____

   _____.

9. Teachers use _____ goals as the basis for planning experiences for children.

## Short Answer (5 points each)
*Complete each exercise.*

10. Give an example of an item that could be included in a child's portfolio.

11. List at least one good source of information about a child with a disability.

12. Why is it important for more than one person to observe a child?

## Multiple Choice (5 points each)
*Check the best response.*

13. The following is an objective and accurate description of a child engaged in an activity.

   ☐ a. Luis ran from the swings to the slide, trying to get there before Britney. He fell, got up, and began whining. He went over to Mrs. Marker.
   ☐ b. Luis ran to the slide, but fell. He started crying because his leg hurt, and he limped to Mrs. Marker.
   ☐ c. Luis was on the swings. He ran toward the slide but fell. He got up, started crying, and limped to Mrs. Marker.
   ☐ d. Luis hurried to slides. On the way, he fell down and seemed to hurt his leg. He got up and cried in pain. He went directly to Mrs. Marker.

14. The following would be a good item to include in a child's portfolio.

   ☐ a. A note the parent sent to the teacher about a minor injury.
   ☐ b. Copies of the child's artwork.
   ☐ c. A copy of the daily schedule.
   ☐ d. A photograph of the child's cubby.

**Extended Answer** (10 points each)

*Complete the following exercises.*

15. Discuss the kinds of questions that teachers ask when evaluating the program at the end of the day.

16. Explain why a team approach to program planning and evaluation is useful.

<table>
<tr><td colspan="2">

**Knowledge Assessment**                          **Module 13: Professionalism**

</td></tr>
</table>

*You may use* Caring for Preschool Children *and your* Skill-Building Journal *to complete this assessment.*

## Matching (5 points each)

*Choose the lettered item in the right column that best matches each statement in the left column. Write the letter of your choice on the line next to the number of the statement.*

| | |
|---|---|
| __ 1. Professional standards guide practice in the early childhood field. Standards define both teacher competence and program quality. | (a) Regularly take advantage of professional development opportunities, such as training workshops and conferences. Learn about current issues and policies in the early childhood field by reading and talking with families and colleagues. |
| __ 2. Teachers continue to grow professionally as they gain experience and refine their skills. It is important for teachers to continue to learn and to keep up-to-date about developmentally appropriate practices. | (b) When a difficult situation arises, consult the Code of Ethical Conduct for guidance on resolving the problem. Be familiar with your program's philosophy and policies, including those regarding conflicts. Attend regular staff meetings to discuss standards, concerns, and ways to resolve problems. |
| __ 3. A code of ethics provides educators with guidelines for acting responsibly and for resolving difficult problems in ways that balance the needs of children, families, and colleagues. | (c) Act on behalf of all children. Share positive experiences and strategies for promoting children's growth and development with families. Stay informed about early childhood policies and pending legislation. Become involved on a state and/or national level. |
| __ 4. An advocate is someone who works for a cause. It is important to share what you know about the needs of young children and about what helps them learn and thrive. | (d) Become familiar with the guidelines for the early childhood field. Make sure you understand developmentally appropriate practice and what expectations and limits are reasonable for the children in your care. |

## Fill in the Blank (5 points each)

*Complete each sentence. Number 5 requires two answers, worth a total of 10 points.*

5.  A professional is a person who has specialized _____

    and _____.

6.  Advocacy means working for _____.

7.  NAEYC issues position statements in order to _____

    _____.

8. Lilian Katz identifies four stages in teaching: survival, consolidation, renewal, and maturity. A teacher at the survival stage would be concerned about _____

_____.

9. Identify one ethical responsibility that early childhood professionals have to their co-workers.

_____

_____.

## Short Answer (5 points each)

*Complete the following exercises.*

10. Identify two of the ways teachers can continue to grow and learn professionally.

11. Explain two of the ways teachers can advocate for children and early childhood programs.

12. How will the early learning standards that states are developing for preschool children help the profession?

13. Give a brief example of how teachers uphold the ethic of treating families respectfully, even in difficult situations.

## Multiple Choice (5 points each)

*Check the response that is the best example or that best completes the sentence.*

14. The following is an example of professional behavior.

- ☐ a. Having all children participate in the same activities at the same time.
- ☐ b. Taking the time to understand why a child is misbehaving.
- ☐ c. Talking about a particular child's behavior in front of that child or other children.
- ☐ d. Making sure that all the children know how to walk in a straight line.

15. Mature teachers are

- ☐ a. over the age of 55.
- ☐ b. teachers who have taught for 20 years or more.
- ☐ c. teachers who realize that children can be expected to work, not play.
- ☐ d. committed professionals who continually seek new ideas, skills, and challenges.

**Extended Answer** (10 points each)

*Complete the following exercises.*

16. Explain why you should talk about the value of your work.

17. Explain how a program can benefit from the accreditation process.

## Knowledge Assessment · Answer Sheets

The Knowledge Assessment for each module is worth a total of 100 points when all questions are answered correctly. A score of 80 points or more is needed to pass the Knowledge Assessment for any module. The questions are scored as follows:

Matching – 5 points each

Fill in the Blank – 5 points for each required answer. Some questions require more than one answer.

Short Answers – 5 points for each required answer. Some questions require more than one answer.

Extended Answer – 10 points each

## Module 1: Safe

### Matching

1. c

2. d

3. a

4. e

5. b

### Fill in the Blank

6. If you know or suspect that a child has been poisoned, immediately call the poison control center, a medical clinic, or 911. (Responses may include any or all of those sources of assistance.)

7. Two important rules to remember when giving first aid are: 1) Do no harm and 2) do not move a child with a serious head, neck, or back injury.

8. When checking a child for injuries, start your examination with the child's head.

### Short Answer

9. Accept any related statement that is expressed in positive terms (i.e., that says what children may do, rather than what they may not do). Examples include, "*Climb outside on the climber,*" or "*Use the step stool to reach the shelf.*"

10. There are many correct answers (e.g., using equipment properly; walking, not running, indoors; using step stools to reach high items; crossing streets at corners and checking for traffic before stepping into the street; using pot holders to handle hot pots and pans; and so on).

11. If a child continues to break a safety rule, remove the child from the situation and explain why he or she is being removed. Direct the child to a new activity that is appropriate to the circumstances.

12. Answers should include two reasons.

   a) Children need quiet activities in order to rest. Most injuries tend to happen when children are tired.

   b) Children need vigorous activity in order to move their bodies. They are less likely to move inappropriately (running inside or climbing on and jumping from furniture) if they have time for active play, both indoors and out.

**Multiple Choice**

13. b

14. d

**Extended Answer**

15. It is important to involve children in setting a few simple rules because they are more likely to understand and remember to follow safety rules that they have helped set.

16. There are many correct answers, such as planning for a children who tires more easily (bring strollers or wagons or plan rest times) or for a child who needs closer supervision (recruit volunteers so the adult:child ratio is larger). Answers should include specific details about what the teacher must anticipate and plan.

# Module 2: Healthy

**Matching**

1. c

2. d

3. e

4. a

5. b

**Fill in the Blank**

6. HIV can be transmitted from mother to child during pregnancy or delivery, through sexual intercourse, by sharing or being stuck with intravenous needles that contain infected blood from a previous user, and from blood and blood product transfusions before 1985.

7. Answers should include two reasons for cooking with preschool children. Accept any reasonable answers, for example, to teach children about nutrition, to promote children's self-help skills, to improve children's fine-motor skills, to increase children's cognitive skills, to provide opportunities for children to socialize, to involve children in sharing the responsibilities of daily living.

8. Mandated reporters are persons who are required by law to report suspected child abuse and neglect.

**Short Answer**

9. Answers may include any aspect of family-style dining, which is discussed on pages 47–48 of *Caring for Preschool Children*.

10. Teachers wash their own hands and help as children wash their hands in order to minimize the spread of infection, to model healthy practice, and to promote children's self-help skills.

11. There are many correct answers. Examples include cleaning table surfaces before and after preparing food; encouraging children to use self-help skills for toileting, handwashing, toothbrushing, and at snack and mealtimes; planning and serving nutritious meals and snacks; helping children recognize when they need rest, movement, food or water; planting a garden; inviting children and providing equipment for them to help maintain a healthy environment; and so on. Suggestions for promoting health habits during interest area activities are provided on pages 50–51 of *Caring for Preschool Children*.

## Multiple Choice

12. c

13. d

14. c

15. c

## Extended Answer

16. Sanitizing surfaces, toys, and equipment; maintaining bathrooms, hygienic food practices, and promoting wellness while children sleep at the center are discussed on pages 32–36 of *Caring for Preschool Children*. Answers should address all classroom areas, not simply toys and tables.

17. Teachers play two key roles in preventing and stopping child abuse and neglect. First, because they care for children daily, they may notice signs of possible abuse and neglect that otherwise might go unnoticed. Second, all states require teachers to report their suspicions of abuse and neglect in accordance with state and local laws. In addition, teachers have an ethical and professional responsibility to keep children safe and to know and follow the reporting requirements and procedures of their state, community, and program. They are also in a position to develop relationships with families and to offer support when it is needed.

# Module 3: Learning Environment

## Matching

1. b

2. d

3. e

4. a

5. c

## Fill in the Blank

6. Transitions are the periods between one activity and the next (or the periods when children move from one activity to the next).

7. There many correct answers, such as a) creating spaces where small groups of children can work together without getting in each other's way, b) providing clear choices so that children can make decisions about what to do and how to do it, c) separating quiet and noisy activities so that children can focus on their play, and d) providing inviting areas where children can get a way from the group when they need time alone. Answers should include two reasons.

8. It is recommended that children have at least 90–120 minutes of outdoor play every day in full-day programs (unless the weather is severe). [Note: If teachers suggest 45–60 minutes, remind them that this is adequate for a single outdoor period but children in full-day programs need to be outside in the morning and the afternoon.]

9. Outdoor space should be organized by types of activities.

## Short Answer

10. There are many correct answers, such as the adaptations listed on pages 74 and 76 of *Caring for Preschool Children*.

11. There are many correct answers, but the response should address the location of the interest area (in relation to other interest areas and to sources of water and electricity), the selection of materials and equipment, and their display. For additional details, see the charts on pages 71–72 and 77–78 of *Caring for Preschool Children*.

## Multiple Choice

12. a

13. b

14. d

15. b

## Extended Answer

16. There are many correct answers, but teachers should mention that children need opportunities and enough time to try their ideas and to become fully involved in their work and play. This includes opportunities to choose what they will do; how they will approach tasks, materials, equipment, and problems; with whom they will play; and when to move to another activity.

17. Tips for smooth transitions are discussed on pages 83–84 of *Caring for Preschool Children*. These include the following ideas:

    - Give children a warning.

    - Involve children in transitional activities.

    - Provide clear directions.

    - Be flexible whenever possible.

    - Allow children to share their work.

    - Keep children occupied.

    - Establish a signal for quiet.

    - Use the time to teach new concepts, practice skills, and encourage creativity.

    Teachers might also mention that following a regular schedule that allows children to learn the order of daily events also helps them transition from one activity to the next.

# Module 4: Physical

## Matching

1. a

2. c

3. d

4. e

5. b

## Fill in the Blank

6. A cue is a word, phrase, or demonstration that helps children perform a task better than the way they are performing it on their own.

7. Three ways to offer cues are by demonstrating (showing), making direct statements, or asking open-ended questions.

8. The best way to know and understand how individual children use their fine and gross motor skills is by observing them.

## Short Answer

9. Accept any reasonable answer that would help a child understand and focus on the component actions of swinging. Correct answers may be statements ("Push your legs out; then tuck them back in."), demonstrating body movements, or guiding questions ("What will happen if you lean backwards a little?").

10. Accept any reasonable answer that indicates an understanding that fine motor development involves increasing hand-eye coordination and control of small muscles.

11. Accept any reasonable answer that indicates an understanding that gross motor development involves children's increasing control of large muscles.

12. Accept any reasonable answer that indicates an understanding that fine and gross motor skills develop along a continuum.

## Multiple Choice

13. b

14. c

## Extended Answer

15. Connections between physical development and other types of development are discussed on pages 94–95 of *Caring for Preschool Children*.

16. There are many correct answers. Continua of fine and gross motor development are outlined on pages 100–101 of *Caring for Preschool Children*.

# Module 5: Cognitive

## Matching

1. d

2. e

3. a

4. b

5. c

## Fill in the Blank

6.  Cognitive development is a child's increasing ability to think and reason.

7.  There are many correct answers that show an understanding that teachers ask questions in order to find out what children know and to encourage children to think and talk about their ideas. Variations of those general responses include ideas such as the following: to learn about children's interests, to find out how children think and try to make sense of their world, to stimulate children's thinking and problem solving, to help children understand how past experiences relate to what is happening now, to help children apply what they have learned to new situations, to engage children in conversation, and to encourage children to find their own answers.

8.  An open-ended question is one that can be answered in a number of different ways.

## Short Answer

9.  Accept any reasonable question that would encourage children to think about what makes things happen (why things happen).

10. Accept any reasonable question that would encourage children to think about what will happen next.

11. Accept any reasonable question that has only one correct answer.

12. Accept answers that are similar to any two of the five following areas of mathematics:

    a)  Exploring number concepts – being able to count and knowing what each number means

    b)  Patterns and relationships – recognizing, creating, and using language to describe regular arrangements that are repeated

    c)  Geometry – recognizing and using language to describe shapes and relationships in space

    d)  Measurement – conceptualizing and using language to describe height, width, length, weight, age, amount, speed, volume, time, and so on

    e)  Collecting and organizing information – identifying, sorting, classifying, grouping, and comparing data

## Multiple Choice

13. c

14. d

15. b

## Extended Answer

16. Explanations of how cognitive development is related to development in other domains are provided on pages 115–116 of *Caring for Preschool Children*.

17. Correct answers discuss the importance of encouraging children's self-confidence as able, active learners. Answers should reflect the idea that cognitive skills include learning how to learn. Children learn best when they can actively question, explore, and research the answers to their questions. The teacher's role is to encourage children's natural interest in exploring and investigating and to encourage them to observe carefully, solve problems, and think for themselves.

# Module 6: Communication

## Matching

1. d

2. e

3. a

4. b

5. c

## Fill in the Blank

6. Accept any reasonable answers that convey the idea that children use language to communicate with others and to learn. Variations include such purposes as to converse, to gain and share information, to talk about events, to express ideas and feelings, to construct understandings, and to listen to and tell stories.

7. Tips for extending children's interest in read-aloud books are listed on page 164 of *Caring for Preschool Children*.

8. Accept any reasonable answer that indicates that teachers are helping children develop concepts about print, e.g., that text carries the message, that print has directionality, that sounds and written symbols correspond, and that written and spoken languages are related.

9. Accept any reasonable answer that indicates that indicates that teachers are helping children develop concepts about print. Answers will probably be very similar to those for question 8.

## Short Answer

10. Strategies for reading aloud to children are listed on page 163 of *Caring for Preschool Children*.

11. Language and communication development alerts are listed on page 144 of *Caring for Preschool Children*.

12. Ideas for including meaningful print in addition to books are listed on pages 150–152. These include dramatic play and block props with writing on them, such as traffic signs, magazines, catalogs, telephone books, grocery advertisements, junk mail, coupons, empty food containers, and menus; posters; charts of the words to songs; recipe cards; age-appropriate software for reading and writing; shelf labels; the daily schedule; signs for each interest area; classroom rules; attendance systems; experience charts; and so on.

## Multiple Choice

13. b

14. b

## Extended Answer

15. Literacy materials for interest areas are discussed on page 150 of *Caring for Preschool Children*.

16. Ideas for arranging the environment to encourage children to listen and speak are outlined on pages 154–155 of *Caring for Preschool Children*.

# Module 7: Creative

## Matching

1.  b

2.  e

3.  d

4.  a

5.  c

## Fill in the Blank

6.  Answers should include two reasons. Correct answers address the general ideas that painting and drawing encourage children to experiment, use their imaginations, and express their feelings and ideas. Variations of that general response include ideas such as the following:

    - Children relax and use all of their senses while they paint and draw.

    - Children make choices without judging right and wrong results.

    - Children experiment with cause and effect and the use of their bodies.

    - Painting and drawing help children refine fine motor skills and coordination.

    - Children explore the properties of different materials; discover what they can do with various tools; and explore concepts about size, color, and shape.

7.  A collage is an art product made by gluing a variety of thin materials on a flat, sturdy surface.

8.  The three key characteristics are a) sensitivity to internal and external stimuli, including increasing awareness of their own emotions; b) lack of inhibition and willingness to experiment and test ideas; and c) complete absorption in engaging activities and the ability to stay involved as long as their interest lasts. Answers do not need to be exhaustive. Other acceptable answers include characteristics such as having vivid imaginations, curiosity, ability to solve problems, increasing ability to manipulate tools and materials, ability to gather and use information, increasing ability to use language for complex dramatic play, willingness to take risks and try new ways of doing things.

## Short Answer

9.  Accept any question that would encourage a child to explore and experiment, i.e., to try a new way of doing something; think about cause and effect; learn from a mistake; respond to art, music, or language; analyze a problem; suggest a solution; express ideas and feelings; make predictions; make comparisons; and so on.

10. The developmental stages of children's art are outlined on page 184 of *Caring for Preschool Children*.

11. Answers should include at least two characteristics. Songs that are good to sing with preschool children have simple words and melodies and are lively and repetitive. Young children also enjoy songs with finger or larger body movements, songs that can become games, and story songs.

## Multiple Choice

12. a

13. a

## Extended Answer

14. There are many correct answers involving arranging the environment to encourage children's exploration and experimentation, offering a variety of materials and activities that promote self-expression, and encouraging and respecting children's ideas. A combination of any of the strategies listed on pages 168–170 of *Caring for Preschool Children* is acceptable, but most answers will probably emphasize the strategies listed on page 170.

15. There are many correct answers. Materials should offer choices but not so many as to overwhelm the children who participate. Teachers should not require the product to look like any other, and their suggestions about how to manipulate tools and materials should encourage children to experiment. Teachers might also mention involving children in cleanup, and they might mention hanging dry paintings at children's eye level, but those ideas are not a required part of the answer.

# Module 8: Self

## Matching

1. c
2. a
3. e
4. b
5. d

## Fill in the Blank

6. *Sense of self* is defined as a person's understanding of who he or she is, how the person identifies him- or herself in terms of culture, environment, physical attributes, preferences, skills, and experiences. Answers may also refer to self-esteem, which is a person's sense of worth and feelings about his or her abilities and accomplishments.

7. In addition to giving all interested children a chance to participate, it is important to repeat activities so that children can practice, master skills, and experience success.

8. Teachers may list any two personality traits. Mentioned on pages 202–203 of *Caring for Preschool Children* are adaptability, intensity, attentiveness, persistence, and resilience.

9. One of the hardest things for teachers to know is when to offer a child help and when to gradually withdraw support so the child can manage independently. Any answer is acceptable that articulates teachers' need to judge when intervention and direction is appropriate and when to stand back so a child can experience the pleasure of working independently. Teachers should tailor their support to meet the needs of individual children in different situations.

10. It is important for teachers to talk with children about their families during the day because it helps children feel connected to their families and tells children that teachers think their families are important. Answers might also include the idea that talking with children about their families gives teachers insights about the children's interests and experiences outside of the program.

## Short Answer

11. Erikson's descriptions of the first three social/emotional stages are outlined on pages 199–200 of *Caring for Preschool Children*.

12. There are many acceptable answers that convey the idea that sharing feelings makes them more manageable. Listening shows respect for children's feelings and helps children learn that teachers are available to help them with their concerns.

13. Teachers invite children to help with meaningful jobs in the classroom so that children feel confident, capable, and part of a community. This helps children develop skills, identify positively with a community, and do things for themselves and others.

## Multiple Choice

14. a

15. c

## Extended Answer

16. Ways teachers can get to know and appreciate each child as an individual are discussed on page 204 of *Caring for Preschool Children*. It is only necessary for teachers to describe one of these ways in their answers.

17. Preschool children tend to talk a lot. Their vocabularies are growing quickly, and they can share ideas, interests, and feelings verbally. They like to talk about themselves and to converse with others. As children become more able to express themselves and use language to understand others, they feel more competent. This sense of competence contributes to a positive sense of self.

# Module 9: Social

## Matching

1. c

2. b

3. a

4. e

5. d

## Fill in the Blank

6. It is important to provide a balance between structured and unstructured activities because children need enough structure to feel secure but they also need opportunities to make choices and interact with each other.

7. A prop box is a collection of items that children can use for dramatic play around a theme that corresponds to their interests or recent experiences.

8. It is important to announce transitions in advance.

9. Their play is cooperative.

10. There are many correct answers, e.g., interpreting children's behavior and labeling feelings (describing in words what the teacher thinks a child is feeling), introducing and repeating the words used to express feelings, sharing one's own feelings when appropriate, reading and discussing stories about coping with feelings and difficult situations, responding to children's needs and requests consistently and as quickly as possible, talking about ways to gain control of strong feelings, providing opportunities for children to play and work with others and coaching them as needed, extending children's dramatic play to include the management of emotions, providing time and encouragement for children to solve their problems and conflicts, include discussion of feelings in daily class meetings, involve children in setting simple rules about respecting themselves and others. Answers only need to identify one strategy.

## Short Answer

11. Strategies for supporting children's efforts to make and keep friends are discussed on pages 236–240 of *Caring for Preschool Children*.

12. There are many correct answers. Routines encourage children to see themselves as members of a community with specific roles and responsibilities. Children can use self-help skills and learn to cooperate as they work together to achieve goals. Routines also help children follow the group's practices.

13. There are many correct answers. Teachers need to overcome their negative feelings about children who are overly aggressive or disruptive because they have an ethical responsibility to value and respect each child, to communicate positively with each child, and not to "discriminate against children…on the basis of their… behavior…" Competent teachers recognize that children's challenging behavior does not make them bad persons. Teachers are better able to help children when they think objectively about the causes of children's challenging behavior. Regardless of the reasons for their behavior, children need a caring adult to help them feel safe and valued.

14. There are many correct answers, such as establishing a concrete system that lets children know when there is room in an interest area for them to play (e.g., five hooks to hang name tags or five pockets in which to place name tags). It also helps to have enough duplicates of popular toys and materials so that children do not have to wait a long time or worry that supplies will be used up.

## Multiple Choice

15. c

16. b

## Extended Answer

17. There are many correct answers. Strategies for guiding and extending children's play are discussed on pages 230–231 of *Caring for Preschool Children*. Answers should describe at least two strategies.

18. There are many correct answers. In addition to the general strategies of modeling appropriate behavior and offering calming activities, teachers might include in their answers the strategies listed on pages 239 and 262 of *Caring for Preschool Children*.

# Module 10: Guidance

## Matching

1. e

2. d

3. a

4. b

5. c

## Fill in the Blank

6. Discipline is often confused with punishment.

7. Effective guidance techniques are based on the developmental and individual characteristics of children.

8. Teachers assume a firm, authoritative role only when necessary to keep children safe.

9. There are several acceptable answers: risks, consequences, or cause and effect.

## Short Answer

10. Acceptable answers indicate that the teacher observes the child to try to discover the cause of the child's distraction and then redirects the child to attempt the activity or to change activities. Answers might also include such strategies as allowing the child to move, planning small-group and time-limited activities, using clear language to give brief instructions, keeping the child near the teacher, limiting external distractions, and so on.

11. There are many correct answers that identify strategies for helping children cooperate, take turns, help others, and manage their emotions. The strategies listed in the *Overview* are acceptable answers, and teachers may cite examples from the text or from their own experience. Answers may be general (e.g., providing opportunities for children to play and work together) or more specific (helping a shy child know what to say in order to join others in play).

12. Possible causes for a child's challenging behavior are listed on pages 260–261. Answers should include three causes.

## Multiple Choice

13. c

14. b

15. a

## Extended Answer

16. There are many correct answers. Answers should indicate that teachers consider developmental and individual characteristics to decide when and how to intervene, whether to ask open-ended questions to help the child determine a new approach, or whether to direct the child to a new activity. Teachers should also evaluate whether classroom activities and materials are interesting and challenging but do not require skills that children do not yet have.

# Module 11: Families

## Matching

1. d

2. a

3. e

4. b

5. c

## Fill in the Blank

6. Families can share their talents, interests, energy, resources, cultures, and so on.

7. Families should not leave the program without saying goodbye to their children.

8. It is helpful to provide a copy of the program's philosophy, policies, schedules, and procedures. (*Family handbook* is also an acceptable answer to this question.)

9. Teachers should be aware of cultural differences that need to be recognized and respected.

## Short Answer

10. *Maintaining confidentiality* means that private information about a person or family will only be shared with persons who have a professional need to know the information.

11. Information that families can offer about their children is discussed on page 265 and on pages 270–273 of *Caring for Preschool Children*. Answers only need to include one type of information.

12. Information that teachers can offer about a child is discussed on page 265 and pages 271–272 of *Caring for Preschool Children*. Answers only need to include one type of information.

13. Sources of long-term stress are listed on pages 288–289 of *Caring for Preschool Children*.

14. Helping families find resources and information about child growth and development is discussed on pages 290–291 of *Caring for Preschool Children*. Answers only need to include one example.

## Multiple Choice

15. b

16. d

## Extended Answer

17. Planning and preparing for conferences is discussed on pages 284–285 of *Caring for Preschool Children*. In their answers, teachers should include flexible scheduling of conferences, reviewing and summarizing information they have collected about each child's progress, organizing work samples to share, thinking about their goals for the child, and encouraging families to consider their goals for the conference.

18. Family participation in classroom activities is discussed on pages 281–283 of *Caring for Preschool Children*. General strategies can be shared with families about how to interact with young children, and specific interest area experiences are listed on page 283. Answers to this question should indicate that teachers orient families to clarify what their responsibilities will be and what they can do to support children's learning.

# Module 12: Program Management

## Matching

1. b
2. c
3. d
4. a

## Fill in the Blank

5. Useful observation notes are complete, accurate, and objective.

6. A program should have a written curriculum to guide teachers' work and an assessment system to determine how each child is progressing.

7. Reasons why teachers observe children are discussed on pages 301–302 of *Caring for Preschool Children*. Answers should include at least two of these reasons: to determine each child's interests, strengths, and needs; to document and report progress; to determine the cause of challenging behavior; and to evaluate the effectiveness of the environment and activities.

8. Children do not behave the same way all of the time, so a single observation cannot provide a complete picture of a child. Many factors affect what children do and say, and children change over time, so observation is an ongoing process.

9. Competent teachers use curriculum goals as the basis for planning experiences for children.

## Short Answer

10. Portfolio items are listed on page 307 of *Caring for Preschool Children*. Correct answers identify items that document the child's work and development.

11. Answers only need to list one source of information: the child, the child's family, doctors, specialists, the child's previous teachers, the child's records, books, journals, the Internet, regional and national support groups, and clearinghouses.

12. It is important for more than one person to observe a child in order to verify objectivity and accurate note taking.

## Multiple Choice

13. c

14. b

## Extended Answer

15. Daily evaluation questions are discussed on page 321 of *Caring for Preschool Children*.

16. Team members each bring different strengths, interests, perspectives, and resources to the planning and evaluation process. The more all team members are involved in the processes, the more likely they are to realize the important role they play in providing a high-quality program.

# Module 13: Professionalism

## Matching

1. d

2. a

3. b

4. c

## Fill in the Blank

5. A professional is a person who has specialized knowledge and skills.

6. Advocacy means working for a cause (or working for change).

7. NAEYC issues position statements in order to explain its organizational thinking about important topics so as to guide and inform early childhood practice.

8. A teacher at the survival stage would be concerned about immediate needs such as learning the program's routines and performing assigned tasks.

9. There are many correct answers related to establishing and maintaining settings and relationships that support productive work and meet professional needs. Variations might include treating colleagues respectfully; being honest, dependable, and regular in attendance; dressing appropriately for work; and advocating on behalf of teachers and early childhood programs.

## Short Answer

10. Ways for teachers to continue to grow and learn professionally are discussed on page 335 and pages 338–339 of *Caring for Preschool Children*. These include joining professional organizations and taking advantage of the print and video materials they offer, reading information on the Internet, joining a study group, attending professional conferences, and participating in training or degree programs. Answers only need to identify two of these ways.

11. Ways for teachers to advocate for children and early childhood programs are listed on pages 346–347 of *Caring for Preschool Children*. Answers only need to include two of these ways.

12. State early learning standards will help the early childhood profession define what preschool children should know and be able to do when they enter kindergarten.

13. There are many acceptable answers that reflect the ethic that teachers should work to bring about collaboration between home and school in ways that enhance the child's development. Answers might address the way that teachers speak with families, maintaining confidentiality, offering support when families are stressed, and jointly finding solutions when conflicts arise.

## Multiple Choice

14. b

15. d

## Extended Answer

16. There are many correct answers. Change is not possible without awareness and understanding, and teachers are in a good position to help others understand the important issues and concerns of the early childhood field. Teachers know a lot about the value of high-quality care and education, children's developmental needs, and the kind of early childhood environments that support children's growth and learning.

17. Programs benefit from the accreditation process because it helps them examine program strengths and weaknesses by assessing environments and practices according to defined standards of quality. It encourages them to address areas of program need and to take pride in areas of program strength.

# Competency Assessment

**Teacher:** _____ **Observer:** _____

**Date/Time:** _____ **Setting:** _____

Review your records from this observation and other information you collected while this teacher was working on module 1. Score each criterion of competence that you can substantiate.

## Maintaining Practices and Environments That Prevent or Reduce Injuries

**The competent teacher will:**

check the appropriate box — met / partially met / not met

1. Check indoor and outdoor areas daily and remove or place out of children's reach any hazardous materials. ☐ ☐ ☐

2. Check the room daily to see that all electrical outlets are covered and electrical cords are placed away from water, traffic paths, and children's reach. ☐ ☐ ☐

3. Check materials and equipment daily for broken parts, loose bolts, or jagged edges; make sure that imperfect materials and equipment are repaired or replaced. ☐ ☐ ☐

4. Arrange the room with clear exit paths and no long or open spaces that tempt children to run. ☐ ☐ ☐

5. Check safety equipment monthly to ensure that it is in good condition and easy to reach. ☐ ☐ ☐

6. Convey to children, in actions and words, that the program is a safe place and that they will be protected. ☐ ☐ ☐

7. Work with colleagues to supervise all children at all times. ☐ ☐ ☐

## Planning for and Responding to Injuries and Emergencies

**The competent teacher will:**

check the appropriate box — met / partially met / not met

8. Develop and post injury and emergency procedures. ☐ ☐ ☐

9. Make sure the telephone is easy to reach and working properly. ☐ ☐ ☐

10. Respond quickly and calmly to children in distress. ☐ ☐ ☐

11. Check the first-aid kit regularly to make sure it has the required supplies. ☐ ☐ ☐

12. Maintain current emergency information for all children. ☐ ☐ ☐

13. Know how to recognize and respond to a medical emergency. ☐ ☐ ☐

14. Know and follow established procedures for leading children to safety during fire and other hazard drills and in real emergencies, and post evacuation routes in each room. ☐ ☐ ☐

## Helping Children Learn to Take Precautions

**The competent teacher will:**

check the appropriate box — met / partially met / not met

15. Take safety precautions in a calm and reassuring manner without overprotecting children or making them fearful. ☐ ☐ ☐

16. Involve children in making safety rules for indoor and outdoor equipment, materials, and activities. ☐ ☐ ☐

17. Remind children of safety rules and emergency procedures by using diagrams, pictures, and words. ☐ ☐ ☐

18. Demonstrate proper ways to use potentially dangerous materials and equipment. ☐ ☐ ☐

19. Teach children to follow safety rules when taking neighborhood walks and study trips. ☐ ☐ ☐

20. Use positive guidance to respond immediately when children are involved in unsafe activities. ☐ ☐ ☐

21. Point out potential hazards so children will learn how to prevent injuries. ☐ ☐ ☐

# Competency Assessment

**Teacher:** _____   **Observer:** _____

**Date/Time:** _____   **Setting:** _____

Review your records from this observation and other information you collected while this teacher was working on module 2. Score each criterion of competence that you can substantiate.

## Maintaining Indoor and Outdoor Environments That Promote Wellness

**The competent teacher will:**

check the appropriate box — met / partially met / not met

1. Check the room daily for adequate ventilation and lighting, comfortable temperature, and sanitary conditions. ☐ ☐ ☐

2. Provide tissues; paper towels; soap; and plastic-lined, covered waste containers within children's reach. ☐ ☐ ☐

3. Complete daily health checks and stay alert to symptoms of illness throughout the day. ☐ ☐ ☐

4. Recognize symptoms of common childhood illnesses, such as strep throat and chicken pox. ☐ ☐ ☐

5. Use the handwashing methods recommended by the Centers for Disease Control and Prevention (CDC) to prevent the spread of germs. ☐ ☐ ☐

6. Clean and disinfect table surfaces before and after preparing and serving food. ☐ ☐ ☐

7. Follow a flexible daily schedule that offers a balance of relaxing and vigorous indoor and outdoor activities. ☐ ☐ ☐

## Helping Children Develop Habits That Promote Good Hygiene and Nutrition

**The competent teacher will:**

check the appropriate box — met / partially met / not met

8. Encourage children to use self-help skills for toileting, handwashing, toothbrushing, and at snack and mealtimes. ☐ ☐ ☐

9. Model healthy habits, such as handwashing, using tissues, eating nutritious foods, and sanitizing materials and surfaces. ☐ ☐ ☐

10. Introduce health and hygiene concepts through daily routines, conversations, books, cooking activities, and visiting health professionals. ☐ ☐ ☐

11. Plan and serve nutritious meals and snacks. ☐ ☐ ☐

12. Sit with children, family-style, during snacks and meals to encourage conversation and to model healthy eating habits. ☐ ☐ ☐

13. Help children recognize when their bodies need rest, food or water, or movement. ☐ ☐ ☐

14. Tell families how you and your colleagues promote wellness. ☐ ☐ ☐

From *A Trainer's Guide to Caring for Preschool Children.*
©2004 Teaching Strategies, Inc., Washington, DC 20015; www.TeachingStrategies.com

## Recognizing and Reporting Child Abuse and Neglect

### The competent teacher will:

check the appropriate box — met — partially met — not met

15. Respond to children in caring ways while avoiding situations that might be questioned by others. ☐ ☐ ☐

16. Know the definitions of physical abuse, sexual abuse, emotional abuse or neglect, and physical neglect. ☐ ☐ ☐

17. Recognize and be alert to the physical and behavioral signs that a child might be a victim of abuse or neglect. ☐ ☐ ☐

18. Report suspected child abuse and neglect to authorities according to applicable laws and program policies. ☐ ☐ ☐

19. Support families by helping them get the services they need. ☐ ☐ ☐

# Competency Assessment

**Teacher:** _____  **Observer:** _____

**Date/Time:** _____  **Setting:** _____

Review your records from this observation and other information you collected while this teacher was working on module 3. Score each criterion of competence that you can substantiate.

## Organizing Indoor and Outdoor Areas That Encourage Play and Exploration

**The competent teacher will:**

| | check the appropriate box | met | partially met | not met |
|---|---|---|---|---|
| 1. Offer a variety of well-defined and equipped indoor and outdoor interest areas. | | ☐ | ☐ | ☐ |
| 2. Create soft, cozy areas where children can get away from the large group. | | ☐ | ☐ | ☐ |
| 3. Organize separate spaces, indoors and outdoors, for active and quiet play. | | ☐ | ☐ | ☐ |
| 4. Make changes to the environment, if necessary, to include children with disabilities. | | ☐ | ☐ | ☐ |
| 5. Provide enough storage for children's personal belongings. | | ☐ | ☐ | ☐ |
| 6. Arrange the outdoor area to support a variety of activities. | | ☐ | ☐ | ☐ |

## Selecting and Displaying Materials and Equipment That Interest and Challenge Children

**The competent teacher will:**

| | check the appropriate box | met | partially met | not met |
|---|---|---|---|---|
| 7. Provide a variety of materials to encourage different kinds of play. | | ☐ | ☐ | ☐ |
| 8. Display learning materials related to children's current interests. | | ☐ | ☐ | ☐ |
| 9. Display materials so children can find and return them independently. | | ☐ | ☐ | ☐ |
| 10. Include materials that reflect diversity. | | ☐ | ☐ | ☐ |
| 11. Store materials and supplies that are used together in the same place. | | ☐ | ☐ | ☐ |
| 12. Display materials in an attractive way. | | ☐ | ☐ | ☐ |

## Planning and Implementing a Schedule and Routines That Support Children's Development and Learning

**The competent teacher will:**

| | check the appropriate box | met | partially met | not met |
|---|---|---|---|---|
| 13. Plan a schedule with large blocks of choice time. | | ☐ | ☐ | ☐ |
| 14. Offer a balance of activity choices. | | ☐ | ☐ | ☐ |
| 15. Plan time each day for children to play outdoors. | | ☐ | ☐ | ☐ |
| 16. Allow time for children to use their self-help skills in daily routines. | | ☐ | ☐ | ☐ |
| 17. Plan for transitions between activities so children won't be bored and restless. | | ☐ | ☐ | ☐ |

# Competency Assessment

**Teacher:** _____   **Observer:** _____

**Date/Time:** _____   **Setting:** _____

Review your records from this observation and other information you collected while this teacher was working on module 4. Score each criterion of competence that you can substantiate.

## Providing Materials, Equipment, and Opportunities for Gross Motor Development

**The competent teacher will:**

check the appropriate box    *met*   *partially met*   *not met*

| | met | partially met | not met |
|---|---|---|---|
| 1. Encourage children to use their large muscles throughout the day. | ☐ | ☐ | ☐ |
| 2. Schedule time for active outdoor play every day. | ☐ | ☐ | ☐ |
| 3. Provide opportunities for active indoor play during bad weather. | ☐ | ☐ | ☐ |
| 4. Encourage the development of self-help skills that involve the use of large muscles. | ☐ | ☐ | ☐ |
| 5. Offer indoor and outdoor activities that challenge children to improve their gross motor skills. | ☐ | ☐ | ☐ |
| 6. Provide a variety of materials and equipment to encourage all children to use their large muscles. | ☐ | ☐ | ☐ |

## Providing Materials and Opportunities for Fine Motor Development

**The competent teacher will:**

check the appropriate box    *met*   *partially met*   *not met*

| | met | partially met | not met |
|---|---|---|---|
| 7. Encourage children to use their small muscles throughout the day. | ☐ | ☐ | ☐ |
| 8. Encourage the development of self-help skills that involve the use of small muscles. | ☐ | ☐ | ☐ |
| 9. Provide a variety of materials that fit together so children can practice their fine motor skills. | ☐ | ☐ | ☐ |
| 10. Provide materials and activities that accommodate different skill levels. | ☐ | ☐ | ☐ |
| 11. Encourage children to participate in daily routines. | ☐ | ☐ | ☐ |

## Reinforcing and Encouraging Children's Physical Development

**The competent teacher will:**

check the appropriate box    *met*   *partially met*   *not met*

| | met | partially met | not met |
|---|---|---|---|
| 12. Offer a variety of materials and activities for different skill levels. | ☐ | ☐ | ☐ |
| 13. Encourage children to coordinate use of their large and small muscles. | ☐ | ☐ | ☐ |
| 14. Help children develop an awareness of rhythm so they can coordinate their body movements. | ☐ | ☐ | ☐ |
| 15. Introduce cooperative games and activities that build children's physical skills. | ☐ | ☐ | ☐ |
| 16. Help older children begin learning skills they can use to play sports and games. | ☐ | ☐ | ☐ |

# Competency Assessment

**Teacher:** _____  **Observer:** _____

**Date/Time:** _____  **Setting:** _____

Review your records from this observation and other information you collected while this teacher was working on module 5. Score each criterion of competence that you can substantiate.

## Creating an Environment That Invites Children to Explore and Investigate

**The competent teacher will:**

check the appropriate box — met / partially met / not met

1. Organize and display toys and materials logically by categories and attributes. ☐ ☐ ☐
2. Provide objects for children to take apart and examine. ☐ ☐ ☐
3. Offer materials that invite children to sort, classify, and order. ☐ ☐ ☐
4. Include living things for children to care for and observe. ☐ ☐ ☐
5. Provide tools children can use to explore and investigate. ☐ ☐ ☐
6. Offer materials that encourage children to explore cause and effect and make predictions. ☐ ☐ ☐

## Interacting With Children in Ways That Stimulate Thinking and Problem Solving

**The competent teacher will:**

check the appropriate box — met / partially met / not met

7. Show children that you respect their work and ideas. ☐ ☐ ☐
8. Comment on children's work in ways that introduce new words and encourage them to extend their ideas. ☐ ☐ ☐
9. Ask questions to help children understand how past experiences relate to what is happening now. ☐ ☐ ☐
10. Point out children's use of logical thinking skills. ☐ ☐ ☐
11. Encourage children to think of several possible answers or solutions. ☐ ☐ ☐
12. Ask questions that help children think about cause and effect and make predictions. ☐ ☐ ☐

## Providing Opportunities for Children to Learn About Their World

**The competent teacher will:**

check the appropriate box — met / partially met / not met

13. Set up activities and provide materials that allow children to test their ideas. ☐ ☐ ☐
14. Build on children's interests and extend their ideas. ☐ ☐ ☐
15. Help children apply what they have learned to new situations. ☐ ☐ ☐
16. Provide books and other resources so children can search for answers to their questions. ☐ ☐ ☐
17. Plan studies on topics that interest children, are worth investigating, and engage them in research. ☐ ☐ ☐
18. Take trips and walks to extend children's understandings about the world. ☐ ☐ ☐

# Competency Assessment

**Teacher:** _____  **Observer:** _____

**Date/Time:** _____  **Setting:** _____

Review your records from this observation and other information you collected while this teacher was working on module 6. Score each criterion of competence that you can substantiate.

## Reading Aloud and Talking With Children About Books, Ideas, and Experiences

**The competent teacher will:**

check the appropriate box — met / partially met / not met

1. Read aloud daily at story time and in response to children's requests. ☐ ☐ ☐
2. Invite children to participate during read-aloud sessions. ☐ ☐ ☐
3. Provide opportunities for children to add to their understandings of a story or topic. ☐ ☐ ☐
4. Offer materials for making books about concepts, topics, and events that are important to the children. ☐ ☐ ☐
5. Encourage family reading and writing times. ☐ ☐ ☐

## Helping Children Focus on the Sounds and Structures of Language

**The competent teacher will:**

check the appropriate box — met / partially met / not met

6. Learn a few words, songs, chants, and rhymes in children's home languages. ☐ ☐ ☐
7. Read aloud books with rhymes, repetition, and silly words. ☐ ☐ ☐
8. Teach children short poems, chants, rhymes, and finger plays. ☐ ☐ ☐
9. Accept every child's way of speaking, while modeling conversational skills and standard use of language. ☐ ☐ ☐
10. Plan activities that focus on the sounds of letters and words. ☐ ☐ ☐

## Encouraging Children to Make Connections Between Speech and Print

**The competent teacher will:**

check the appropriate box — met / partially met / not met

11. Provide a print-rich environment that shows how written language is used to communicate. ☐ ☐ ☐
12. Create comfortable, well-stocked library and writing areas. ☐ ☐ ☐
13. Post charts and lists with words and pictures that ask children to provide and organize information. ☐ ☐ ☐
14. Encourage children to communicate ideas and requests through pictures and writing. ☐ ☐ ☐
15. Show children how adults use reading and writing. ☐ ☐ ☐
16. Select and display a variety of books. ☐ ☐ ☐

# Competency Assessment

**Teacher:** _____  **Observer:** _____

**Date/Time:** _____  **Setting:** _____

Review your records from this observation and other information you collected while this teacher was working on module 7. Score each criterion of competence that you can substantiate.

## Arranging the Environment to Encourage Exploration and Experimentation

**The competent teacher will:**                              check the appropriate box  met  partially met  not met

1. Display and store materials within children's reach on open shelves that are no taller than 3 feet. ☐ ☐ ☐

2. Offer spaces where children can explore, make noise, move their bodies, and be messy. ☐ ☐ ☐

3. Provide protected spaces where children may save both finished and unfinished creations. ☐ ☐ ☐

4. Help children display their work attractively. ☐ ☐ ☐

5. Display interesting pictures and objects within reach and invite children to explore them. ☐ ☐ ☐

6. Adapt the schedule, when appropriate, so children have enough time to act on their ideas. ☐ ☐ ☐

## Offering a Variety of Materials and Activities That Promote Self-Expression

**The competent teacher will:**                              check the appropriate box  met  partially met  not met

7. Assess the children's current interests and provide a variety of appropriate materials, props, and objects. ☐ ☐ ☐

8. Offer materials, props, and objects that reflect the cultures and ethnicities of all children in the class. ☐ ☐ ☐

9. Plan activities and ask questions that encourage children to use their imaginations. ☐ ☐ ☐

10. Provide a variety of materials for children to use in different ways depending on their interests, ideas, and plans. ☐ ☐ ☐

11. Offer messy open-ended activities such as finger painting; bubble blowing; and water, sand, and mud play. ☐ ☐ ☐

## Encouraging and Respecting Children's Ideas

**The competent teacher will:**

check the appropriate box — met — partially met — not met

12. Invite children to express their ideas and feelings. ☐ ☐ ☐

13. Extend and expand children's dramatic play by assuming pretend roles or offering a new prop. ☐ ☐ ☐

14. Show respect for the creative process as well as the creative product. ☐ ☐ ☐

15. Ask open-ended questions that encourage children to solve problems and think in new ways. ☐ ☐ ☐

16. Accept and value each child's unique ideas and expressions. ☐ ☐ ☐

Teaching Strategies. From *A Trainer's Guide to Caring for Preschool Children.*
©2004 Teaching Strategies, Inc., Washington, DC 20015; www.TeachingStrategies.com
**165**

# Competency Assessment

**Teacher:** _____  **Observer:** _____

**Date/Time:** _____  **Setting:** _____

Review your records from this observation and other information you collected while this teacher was working on module 8. Score each criterion of competence that you can substantiate.

## Helping Children Learn About Themselves and Others

**The competent teacher will:**

check the appropriate box — met / partially met / not met

1. Offer a bias-free program that respects differences such as gender, ability, culture, ethnicity, and family background. ☐ ☐ ☐

2. Provide opportunities for children to learn about and appreciate people of different cultures and ethnic groups. ☐ ☐ ☐

3. Encourage children to share and build on their interests. ☐ ☐ ☐

4. Show appreciation for children's positive behavior. ☐ ☐ ☐

5. Learn and use a few words in the home languages of children whose first language is not English. ☐ ☐ ☐

6. Encourage children to talk about their feelings and take their concerns seriously. ☐ ☐ ☐

## Respecting Each Child as an Individual

**The competent teacher will:**

check the appropriate box — met / partially met / not met

7. Observe each child regularly to learn about individual needs, skills, abilities, interests, culture, and family experiences. ☐ ☐ ☐

8. Know what each child can do and show that you value individual interests and abilities. ☐ ☐ ☐

9. Offer verbal and gentle nonverbal contact to show you care about the child's well-being. ☐ ☐ ☐

10. Spend individual time with each child every day. ☐ ☐ ☐

11. Help children learn how to handle their strong feelings. ☐ ☐ ☐

12. Show by what you say and do that you respect each child. ☐ ☐ ☐

## Providing a Program That Enables Children to Be Successful

**The competent teacher will:**

check the appropriate box    *met*   *partially met*   *not met*

13. Provide a range of activities and materials that can be enjoyed by children with varied interests, abilities, and skills. ☐ ☐ ☐

14. Acknowledge children's efforts as well as their accomplishments. ☐ ☐ ☐

15. Allow children to do as much as possible for themselves, even if they take a long time. ☐ ☐ ☐

16. Repeat activities so children can practice, master skills, and experience success. ☐ ☐ ☐

17. Accept mistakes as a natural part of learning. ☐ ☐ ☐

18. Consider children's individual characteristics when setting up the environment, choosing materials, and planning activities. ☐ ☐ ☐

# Competency Assessment

**Teacher:** _____  **Observer:** _____

**Date/Time:** _____  **Setting:** _____

Review your records from this observation and other information you collected while this teacher was working on module 9. Score each criterion of competence that you can substantiate.

## Offering a Program That Helps Children Develop Social Skills

**The competent teacher will:**

check the appropriate box — met / partially met / not met

1. Include large blocks of time in the daily schedule when children may choose their play activities and partners. ☐ ☐ ☐

2. Hold daily class meetings. ☐ ☐ ☐

3. Plan classroom jobs and routines so two or more children can work together. ☐ ☐ ☐

4. Involve children in setting a few simple rules about respecting themselves, each other, and the toys and materials. ☐ ☐ ☐

5. Provide materials and activities that encourage two or more children to play together. ☐ ☐ ☐

6. Introduce children to the community beyond the classroom and program. ☐ ☐ ☐

## Teaching Children the Skills to Play and Learn With Others

**The competent teacher will:**

check the appropriate box — met / partially met / not met

7. Model caring behavior. ☐ ☐ ☐

8. Provide time and encouragement for children to solve their problems and conflicts. ☐ ☐ ☐

9. Join in children's play by following their lead. ☐ ☐ ☐

10. Read and discuss stories about coping with feelings and difficult situations. ☐ ☐ ☐

11. Point out and endorse children's positive solutions to their problems. ☐ ☐ ☐

12. Share your own feelings when appropriate. ☐ ☐ ☐

## Building a Positive Relationship With Each Child

**The competent teacher will:**

check the appropriate box — met / partially met / not met

13. Describe in words what you think a child is feeling. ☐ ☐ ☐

14. Introduce and repeat the words used to express feelings. ☐ ☐ ☐

15. Assist a child who has difficulty joining a group at play. ☐ ☐ ☐

16. Respond to individual needs and requests consistently and as quickly as possible. ☐ ☐ ☐

17. Help a child understand the potential and actual consequences of certain behavior. ☐ ☐ ☐

From *A Trainer's Guide to Caring for Preschool Children.*
©2004 Teaching Strategies, Inc., Washington, DC 20015; www.TeachingStrategies.com

# Competency Assessment

**Teacher:** _____     **Observer:** _____

**Date/Time:** _____     **Setting:** _____

Review your records from this observation and other information you collected while this teacher was working on module 10. Score each criterion of competence that you can substantiate.

## Minimizing Problem Behavior and Encouraging Self-Discipline

**The competent teacher will:**

check the appropriate box — met | partially met | not met

| | met | partially met | not met |
|---|---|---|---|
| 1. Provide open-ended materials and activities that support varied interests and skills. | ☐ | ☐ | ☐ |
| 2. Establish a comfortable setting that looks and feels like children's homes. | ☐ | ☐ | ☐ |
| 3. Create cozy spaces where a child can be alone for awhile, yet still be visible to adults. | ☐ | ☐ | ☐ |
| 4. Follow a schedule that allows children to choose their own activities for most of the day. | ☐ | ☐ | ☐ |
| 5. Arrange the room so traffic paths, interest areas, and the large group area are clearly defined. | ☐ | ☐ | ☐ |
| 6. Provide materials and activities that allow children to explore and express their feelings. | ☐ | ☐ | ☐ |

## Using Positive Guidance to Help Each Child Learn Acceptable Behavior

**The competent teacher will:**

check the appropriate box — met | partially met | not met

| | met | partially met | not met |
|---|---|---|---|
| 7. Build trusting, supportive relationships with individual children. | ☐ | ☐ | ☐ |
| 8. Work with colleagues to make sure all of the children have ongoing, positive interactions with their teachers. | ☐ | ☐ | ☐ |
| 9. Teach problem-solving skills and help children apply them to negotiate and resolve disagreements. | ☐ | ☐ | ☐ |
| 10. Involve the children in setting a few important rules. | ☐ | ☐ | ☐ |
| 11. Redirect children to acceptable alternative activities. | ☐ | ☐ | ☐ |
| 12. Use simple, positive reminders that tell children what to do, rather than what not to do. | ☐ | ☐ | ☐ |
| 13. Assume a firm, authoritarian role only when necessary to keep children safe. | ☐ | ☐ | ☐ |
| 14. Model appropriate ways to identify and express feelings. | ☐ | ☐ | ☐ |

## Helping Children Express Their Strong Feelings in Acceptable Ways

**The competent teacher will:**

check the
appropriate box    *met*   *partially met*   *not met*

15. Look for the reasons why a child might behave inappropriately.    ☐ ☐ ☐

16. Acknowledge frustrating experiences and suggest ways to cope with them.    ☐ ☐ ☐

17. Identify and discuss feelings and suggest appropriate ways to express them.    ☐ ☐ ☐

18. Help children understand the causes and effects of their actions on people and things.    ☐ ☐ ☐

19. Work with a family to help a child with challenging behavior learn acceptable ways to express strong feelings.    ☐ ☐ ☐

From *A Trainer's Guide to Caring for Preschool Children.*
©2004 Teaching Strategies, Inc., Washington, DC 20015; www.TeachingStrategies.com

# Competency Assessment

**Teacher:** _____    **Observer:** _____

**Date/Time:** _____    **Setting:** _____

Review your records from this observation and other information you collected while this teacher was working on module 11. Score each criterion of competence that you can substantiate.

## Communicating Frequently With Families to Share Information About Their Children and the Program

**The competent teacher will:**

|  | check the appropriate box | met | partially met | not met |
|---|---|---|---|---|
| 1. Share information with families on a daily basis. | | ☐ | ☐ | ☐ |
| 2. Respond to families' questions and concerns. | | ☐ | ☐ | ☐ |
| 3. Keep families informed about program activities. | | ☐ | ☐ | ☐ |
| 4. Get to know a little about each family. | | ☐ | ☐ | ☐ |
| 5. Tailor communication strategies to meet individual needs. | | ☐ | ☐ | ☐ |
| 6. Hold parent-teacher conferences regularly and as needed to share information about children's progress and to plan. | | ☐ | ☐ | ☐ |

## Offering a Variety of Ways for Families to Participate in the Program

**The competent teacher will:**

|  | check the appropriate box | met | partially met | not met |
|---|---|---|---|---|
| 7. Invite family members to visit the program at any time. | | ☐ | ☐ | ☐ |
| 8. Make participation in the classroom a positive experience for family members. | | ☐ | ☐ | ☐ |
| 9. Invite families to share talents, interests, and aspects of their culture. | | ☐ | ☐ | ☐ |
| 10. Offer workshops and resources on topics of interest to families. | | ☐ | ☐ | ☐ |
| 11. Hold meetings and events at times that are convenient for most families. | | ☐ | ☐ | ☐ |
| 12. Offer a variety of ways for families to contribute to the program. | | ☐ | ☐ | ☐ |

## Providing Support to Families

**The competent teacher will:**

|  | check the appropriate box | met | partially met | not met |
|---|---|---|---|---|
| 12. Maintain confidentiality about children and families. | | ☐ | ☐ | ☐ |
| 13. Recognize when families are under stress and offer additional support. | | ☐ | ☐ | ☐ |
| 14. Work with families to develop strategies for promoting children's positive behavior. | | ☐ | ☐ | ☐ |
| 15. Help families understand what their children learn through daily routines and activities. | | ☐ | ☐ | ☐ |
| 16. Use familiar terms instead of professional jargon when talking with families. | | ☐ | ☐ | ☐ |
| 17. Provide families with information on child development and typical preschool behavior. | | ☐ | ☐ | ☐ |
| 18. Notify a supervisor when a family seems to need professional help. | | ☐ | ☐ | ☐ |

# Competency Assessment

**Teacher:** _____  **Observer:** _____

**Date/Time:** _____  **Setting:** _____

Review your records from this observation and other information you collected while this teacher was working on module 12. Score each criterion of competence that you can substantiate.

## Collecting Information About Each Child

**The competent teacher will:**

check the appropriate box — met / partially met / not met

1. Communicate with parents often, using a variety of strategies. ☐ ☐ ☐

2. Observe each child regularly and use a notation system that is objective, accurate, and avoids labeling. ☐ ☐ ☐

3. Observe children in different settings and at different times of the day. ☐ ☐ ☐

4. Collect examples and photographs of work that document children's skills, interests, and progress. ☐ ☐ ☐

5. Play and talk with children to learn about their interests and abilities. ☐ ☐ ☐

## Working as a Team to Offer an Individualized Program

**The competent teacher will:**

check the appropriate box — met / partially met / not met

6. Meet regularly with colleagues to plan the program. ☐ ☐ ☐

7. Ensure that curriculum goals are the basis for planning experiences for the children. ☐ ☐ ☐

8. Use ongoing assessment information to plan for individual children and the group. ☐ ☐ ☐

9. Include each family in planning how to encourage their children's development and learning. ☐ ☐ ☐

10. Use creative thinking skills, such as brainstorming, to plan and solve problems. ☐ ☐ ☐

11. Appreciate and use the strengths of all team members, including teachers, families, and volunteers. ☐ ☐ ☐

## Using Information to Evaluate the Program

**The competent teacher will:**

check the appropriate box — met / partially met / not met

12. Use program goals as a component of the program evaluation. ☐ ☐ ☐

13. Identify what is working well and what needs to be improved, every day. ☐ ☐ ☐

14. Plan teaching approaches and change the environment, materials, interest areas, routines, and activities in response to what you learn about each child. ☐ ☐ ☐

15. Use information about children's use of materials to determine if changes are needed. ☐ ☐ ☐

From *A Trainer's Guide to Caring for Preschool Children.*
©2004 Teaching Strategies, Inc., Washington, DC 20015; www.TeachingStrategies.com

# Notes

# Appendix

# Module-Completion Plan

Review your responses to the *Self-Assessment* with your trainer. What do you think are your strengths, interests, and needs? Decide which areas you would like to work on first. Select three modules to begin with and set target dates for their completion. (Your trainer can let you know how much work is involved for each module.) Record the module titles and target completion dates below. You may also wish to determine a tentative schedule for completing *Caring for Preschool Children*.

| Module | Target Completion Date |
|--------|------------------------|
|        |                        |

Tentative schedule for completion of the *Caring for Preschool Children* Training Program:

| Module | Date |
|--------|------|
|        |      |

**Teacher:**_____ **Date:**_____ **Trainer:**_____ **Date:**_____

Teaching Strategies. From *A Trainer's Guide to Caring for Preschool Children.*
©2004 Teaching Strategies, Inc., Washington, DC 20015; www.TeachingStrategies.com

# Planning Form for Group Sessions

**Module:** _____

Use this form to plan a series of group sessions on a module. Tailor your plan to address individual interests and training needs.

## Overview, Your Own Experiences, and Pre-Training Assessment

1. Open the session.  Greet participants. Return completed forms with your comments and give teachers time to review them. Begin a dialogue by asking an open-ended question.

   _____

   _____

   _____

   _____

   _____

   _____

2. Discuss the module topic.
   Introduce the three areas of competence related to the module topic.

   _____

   _____

   _____

   _____

   _____

   Lead a discussion by posing questions that will encourage participation.

   _____

   _____

   _____

   _____

   _____

# Planning Form for Group Sessions, continued

3.  Review the three examples in the overview.

    Discuss the example situations and teachers' responses to the questions. Ask participants to describe similar experiences and their own practices. Ask questions such as:

    - What do you think about the way the teacher handled the situation?
    - How would you handle a similar situation in your program?

    _____

    _____

    _____

    _____

    _____

    _____

4.  Discuss the section on teachers' personal experiences.

    _____

    _____

    _____

    _____

    _____

    _____

5.  End the session.

    Answer questions. Schedule individual meetings or phone conferences to discuss responses and the 3–5 skills and topics teachers want to learn more about.

# Planning Form for Group Sessions, continued

**Learning Activity*:**_____

1. Open the session.

   Greet participants. Return completed learning activity forms with your comments and give teachers time to review them. Begin a dialogue by asking an open-ended question, reviewing the previous learning activity, or discussing a follow-up assignment from the previous meeting.

   _____

   _____

   _____

   _____

   _____

   _____

2. Discuss the text.

   Lead a discussion about the key points presented in the learning activity.

   _____

   _____

   _____

   _____

   _____

   _____

3. Review the activity.

   Ask participants to describe their experiences completing this learning activity. Encourage them to share examples from their work with children, families, and colleagues.

   _____

   _____

   _____

   _____

   _____

   _____

---

\* Complete one plan for each learning activity in this module.

4. Offer additional resources and activities.

   List any materials, audiovisual resources, topics for discussion, or exercises you will use to supplement the learning activity.

   _____

   _____

   _____

   _____

   _____

5. End the session.

   Introduce the next learning activity.

   _____

   _____

   _____

   _____

   _____

   Offer to review and discuss the activity during individual meetings or phone conferences.

   Remind participants of the time and place for your next session and when to submit their completed learning activity forms for your review and written comments.

   If this is the last session for this module, also discuss *Reflecting on Your Learning*.

   Return completed progress summaries with your comments. Offer to review and discuss them during individual meetings or phone conferences.

   Ask teachers to share one idea that they learned while working on this module.

   Invite teachers to describe some of the ways they adapted or changed their practices related to the topic addressed in the module.

   Schedule individual meetings with teachers to review their progress and schedule the knowledge and competency assessments.

# Individual Tracking Form

**Name:** _____

**Date Completed:** _____

| Module | Overview | Self-Assessment | Pre-Training Assessment | Your Own Experiences | Learning Activity A | Learning Activity B | Learning Activity C | Learning Activity D | Learning Activity E | Reflecting on Your Learning | Knowledge Assessment | Competency Assessment | Trainer Sign-off |
|---|---|---|---|---|---|---|---|---|---|---|---|---|---|
| Orientation | X | | X | X | X | X | X | X | X | X | X | X | |
| 1. Safe | | X | | | | | | | X | | | | |
| 2. Healthy | | X | | | | | | | | | | | |
| 3. Learning Environment | | X | | | | | | | X | | | | |
| 4. Physical | | X | | | | | | | X | | | | |
| 5. Cognitive | | X | | | | | | | X | | | | |
| 6. Communication | | X | | | | | | | X | | | | |
| 7. Creative | | X | | | | | | | X | | | | |
| 8. Self | | X | | | | | | | X | | | | |
| 9. Social | | X | | | | | | | | | | | |
| 10. Guidance | | X | | | | | | | | | | | |
| 11. Families | | X | | | | | | | | | | | |
| 12. Program Management | | X | | | | | | | X | | | | |
| 13. Professionalism | | X | | | | | | | X | | | X | |

# Program Tracking Form

## Modules

| Teachers | Orientation | | Safe | | Healthy | | Learning Environment | | Physical | | Cognitive | | Communication | | Creative | | Self | | Social | | Guidance | | Families | | Program Management | | Professionalism | |
|---|---|---|---|---|---|---|---|---|---|---|---|---|---|---|---|---|---|---|---|---|---|---|---|---|---|---|---|---|
| | B | C | B | C | B | C | B | C | B | C | B | C | B | C | B | C | B | C | B | C | B | C | B | C | B | C | B | C |
| | | | | | | | | | | | | | | | | | | | | | | | | | | | | |
| | | | | | | | | | | | | | | | | | | | | | | | | | | | | |
| | | | | | | | | | | | | | | | | | | | | | | | | | | | | |
| | | | | | | | | | | | | | | | | | | | | | | | | | | | | |
| | | | | | | | | | | | | | | | | | | | | | | | | | | | | |
| | | | | | | | | | | | | | | | | | | | | | | | | | | | | |
| | | | | | | | | | | | | | | | | | | | | | | | | | | | | |
| | | | | | | | | | | | | | | | | | | | | | | | | | | | | |
| | | | | | | | | | | | | | | | | | | | | | | | | | | | | |
| | | | | | | | | | | | | | | | | | | | | | | | | | | | | |
| | | | | | | | | | | | | | | | | | | | | | | | | | | | | |
| | | | | | | | | | | | | | | | | | | | | | | | | | | | | |
| | | | | | | | | | | | | | | | | | | | | | | | | | | | | |
| | | | | | | | | | | | | | | | | | | | | | | | | | | | | |
| | | | | | | | | | | | | | | | | | | | | | | | | | | | | |

**B= Begun    C=Completed**

From *A Trainer's Guide to Caring for Preschool Children.*
©2004 Teaching Strategies, Inc., Washington, DC 20015; www.TeachingStrategies.com

# Training Record

**Name:** _____

**Program:** _____

| Topic | Date(s) | Hours | Type of Training (conference, course, workshop, observation/feedback) | Agency Providing Training | Signature of Trainer |
|---|---|---|---|---|---|
| | | | | | |
| | | | | | |
| | | | | | |
| | | | | | |
| | | | | | |
| | | | | | |

From *A Trainer's Guide to Caring for Preschool Children.*
©2004 Teaching Strategies, Inc., Washington, DC 20015; www.TeachingStrategies.com

185

# CERTIFICATE of COMPLETION

## AWARDED TO

_____

for completion of _____ hours of training on

*Caring for Preschool Children, 3rd Edition*

20____

Verification of Training may be obtained from:

Agency Sponsoring Training: _____

Sponsor's Address: _____

City/ State/ Zip: _____

Sponsor's Phone Number: (____) _____

_____
(Trainer's Signature)

*caring for*
**preschool**
**children** third edition

# Training Evaluation Form

**Session Title:**_____  **Date:**_____

**Trainer:**_____

|  | check the appropriate box | completely | somewhat | not at all |
|---|---|---|---|---|

## A. Content

1. Did the topics address your needs? ☐ ☐ ☐
2. Was the information relevant to your job? ☐ ☐ ☐

## B. Trainer

3. Was the trainer well-informed on the subjects? ☐ ☐ ☐
4. Did the trainer help you learn? ☐ ☐ ☐
5. Was the presentation well-organized? ☐ ☐ ☐

## C. Materials

6. How appropriate and usable were the handouts? ☐ ☐ ☐
7. How appropriate were other resources such as videos? ☐ ☐ ☐

## D. Suggestions or Comments *(Indicate your likes, dislikes, and recommendations.)*

## E. How will you apply what you learned in this training?

**Your name (optional):** _____

Teaching Strategies. From *A Trainer's Guide to Caring for Preschool Children.*
©2004 Teaching Strategies, Inc., Washington, DC 20015; www.TeachingStrategies.com

# Notes

# Notes

# Notes

# Notes

# Notes

# Notes

# Notes

# Notes

# Notes

# Notes

# Notes